FALAFELS AND BEDOUINS

A holiday travel memoir of Israel and Jordan

NOOR DE OLINAD

ISBN: 978-0-9925520-5-3 (EPUB)

ISBN: 978-0-9925520-6-0 (MOBIpocket)

ISBN: 978-0-9925520-7-7 (PRINT)

❀ Created with Vellum

PREFACE

This travel memoir is a snapshot of Israel in 2012 and not intended as a practical travel guide. If I were to recount every detail of my trip, this would be a very long book indeed. Instead, for your enjoyment and my sanity, I have cut out the boring bits and kept the most entertaining and touching moments, recreating events and dialogue from memory. Names of places were retained, but I changed names of mentioned individuals to protect their anonymity.

The Middle East is a fascinating part of the world and I wanted to share my experiences to amuse and inform other travellers, especially inexperienced ones like me.

CHAPTER 1
ARE WE THERE YET?

I scrolled through the list of movies available for the flight.

"I'm surprised you're not learning more Hebrew," Emily said, flicking through a magazine.

"Can't concentrate with that baby crying. Did you remember to ask for vegan food?"

"Yep. I still can't believe we're on our way to Israel and Jordan!"

I looked at my friend and work colleague. If it wasn't for her, I wouldn't be on the plane right now. It had been her idea to travel together. She wanted to explore her Jewish roots and I wanted somewhere exciting and exotic to escape from my soul crushing, dead end job. Somewhere as different to my everyday reality as possible. Plus, Petra and Jerusalem had been on my bucket list for years.

"I'm excited, but to be completely honest also a little nervous. We're two single women, travelling alone in the Middle East. I think we'll be fine in the big cities in Israel, but I don't know much about the culture in Jordan …"

Emily nodded, her dark eyes serious. "That's why I'm glad you wanted to go to Petra too. We'll be safer travelling together. And bonus – you know a lot about Jewish and Middle Eastern culture, so you can be our tour guide!"

"Ha! I don't know about that. My thesis research was at a small synagogue, so I'm not some expert or anything. But as far as Middle Eastern culture, I definitely know a lot about the delicious food."

"Ooooh, I'm looking forward to trying some authentic falafels! It's going to be great – well, once we eventually get there."

"I didn't think it would be so difficult organizing this trip," I said. "I had no idea there isn't a direct flight from Australia to Israel, did you?"

"No, but that explains why our flight tickets are so expensive."

I cringed. $3,000 AUD just for the flight because we had to change planes in Dubai, fly to Jordan and then, finally, catch a connecting flight from Amman to Tel Aviv.

"Lucky we found that cheap hotel in Jerusalem," I said, adjusting my neck pillow.

"And it's in an amazing location with a rooftop terrace!"

I grinned. The hotel had been a lucky find. There were plenty of religious houses to choose from in Jerusalem, but as neither of us was religious we opted for a regular hotel and this one stood out from the rest. It was a 400 year old building in the heart of Jerusalem, near the Via Dolorosa, marketplaces and the Dome of the Rock. The best part was, it was within our budget!

Emily pointed at the paper sticking out of my backpack. "Have you finished planning our itinerary for Jerusalem?"

I nodded and pulled out the colour coded, day-by-day plan I had spent hours making. "It will be busy, but this way we'll see most of Jerusalem."

"Sounds good. I'll read the maps, and you can translate for us."

I laughed. "I'm not that good. I've only managed to learn basic greetings and some phrases. I can say *Kamah Zeh Oleh?* and *Eifo HaSherutim?*"

"What does that mean?"

"How much does that cost and where are the bathrooms?"

"I'm sure we'll be fine," Emily chuckled. "Anyway, it's only for four days. When we join the tour group, we can take it easy." She smoothed her wavy black hair and closed her eyes. "I'm going to try and get some sleep."

"Good idea."

I reclined my seat, closed my eyes and put on classical music to drown out the baby's non-stop crying. Instead of sleep, a wave of guilt and nostalgia washed over me.

I hope grandma and my cousins will understand. I know I promised I would go back to Italy, but I might not get another chance to visit the Middle East.

The guilt didn't go away. I knew grandma and cousin Amalia were getting older, but I could go to Italy next year. I'd finished university and I had a job now, so it wouldn't take me as long to save money for the trip. My relatives in Italy weren't the only ones I felt guilty about.

I didn't like leaving my cat Susu and dog Brûlê (also lovingly known as Susi and Bruli), even when I knew that my parents and sister would spoil them completely. I couldn't help chuckling softly, picturing dad trying to watch TV with Susu asleep on his chest and Brûlê insisting on being patted.

My parents and sister had made me promise to email them regularly. I knew it wasn't just my choice of destination that worried them. This was the first time I was travelling since my diagnosis of Addison's disease.

My eyes flew open and I bent over to re-check my medical kit.

Emergency injection kit – check.

Enough tablets for a month – check.

I leaned back in my chair but couldn't relax. All the things that could possibly go wrong kept going round and round in my mind; catching a virus, developing a fever, getting food poisoning, running out of medication… To a healthy person, all manageable problems. To me, any one of those could make me severely ill and land me in hospital. If I was very unlucky, I could end up in a coma.

Stop it! I'm going to be FINE!

I forced my eyes closed again and tried to focus on the music coming from my headphones. Emily knew what symptoms to look out for if I were to go into an Addisonian crisis, and if necessary, she was prepared to try and give me my injection. I crossed my fingers and desperately hoped it wouldn't come to that.

The music stood no chance against the baby's piercing cries. Sighing, I sat up and selected an action packed Hollywood movie.

I'll sleep when the baby does, I thought in resignation.

As soon as the aeroplane wheels touched the ground, the passengers around us stood and retrieved their luggage from the over-head compartment. While the seat belt sign was still on, they started edging forward towards the exits. We waited for the plane to stop moving before collecting our hand luggage, and consequently were among the last few passengers to disembark.

"We should hurry," I said to Emily, dodging flying elbows as people rushed past us. "We don't have long to catch our connecting flight and we have no idea where it is."

"I think it's in that direction," Emily indicated.

We set off at a brisk pace, dragging our hand luggage behind. We walked past an entire wall covered in brilliantly shiny and thick 18 carat gold jewellery for sale, and past the smoking lounge (a glass room with a dense cloud of smoke, revealing only serious looking business shoes and spiky high heels). You could practically feel some kind of smoke related cancer growing just by looking at it, but I had more immediate concerns to worry about.

There were no signs indicating where to catch the connection flight, no one who really spoke English and those that did, answered questions with no hint of a smile or friendliness.

The guards at the check-in were, putting it politely... brusque. It was all very serious with soldiers walking around armed with rifles, while people were being passed through metal detectors and searched. After walking in the wrong direction for a while, hoping to see a sign indicating where to go, we came across a flight attendant from the airline we were flying with.

"Let's ask her," Emily suggested. "She probably knows where the information desk is."

"Excuse me," I called out and was relieved when she stopped. "Could you tell us where the information desk is? We can't find where to go to catch our connection flight."

Immaculately dressed in her uniform and wearing bright red lipstick, she gave us a friendly smile.

"May I see your boarding pass?" she asked in lightly accented English.

I handed her my documents and hoped she could point us in the right direction.

"I am going in that direction now. You can follow me if you like," she offered.

"Thank you very much!" Emily said.

"We must catch elevator," the hostess indicated to the small glass box behind her.

Somehow, the three of us and our hand luggage managed to fit.

"Jordan is beautiful, how long you will stay there?" the hostess asked, still smiling.

"Actually, we are heading to Israel but have to catch a connection flight from Jordan to get there," Emily explained.

The smile dropped from the air hostess's face. "You are going to *Israel*?"

"Yes, we booked a tour and after that we will go to Jordan to see Petra," I clarified.

She didn't speak to us again except to say, "Follow me"

and "Your boarding gate is that way," before leaving us, with no hint of the friendly smile from earlier.

Maybe we should be more discreet about our travel destination while making our way to Israel, I thought, feeling a little nervous.

I knew that Israel often had tense relations with its neighbours, but we were tourists and the political situation in the Middle East had nothing to do with us. Surely it was my own personal business where I chose to spend my holidays?

Well, whatever the air hostess thought or felt about my travel destination, I was grateful she had taken us to the correct area for boarding.

EMILY TOOK her heat by the window, which left me in the middle next to a very active 6 year old boy and a tired looking woman I assumed was his mother. He undid his seat belt as soon as it was on, stood on the chair and played with the hair of the woman in front. When his mother sat him down, he started kicking the chair in front then pulled out my headphones and draped himself over my lap. His mother pleaded with him to behave, trying to sit him up properly but he wailed and slapped her face. She was busy apologizing to everyone around her when the air hostess came.

"Madam, your son needs to sit in the chair and have his seat belt on," the air hostess told her.

"He doesn't want to," the woman said apologetically.

"It's not safe! I will try." said the air hostess.

She tried to bribe, then scold the little boy into putting on his seat belt. Every time they managed to get him into the chair, he screamed and screamed.

"Please control your child," the air hostess said through gritted teeth.

"Not mine, I am nanny," the woman said. "His older sister there, maybe listen to her."

We all looked at the teenage girl she pointed to, obliviously watching a movie.

The air hostess walked over and tapped her on the shoulder. "Is that your little brother?"

The girl nodded.

"He must sit and put his seat belt on," the air hostess told her. "He is not listening to his nanny, so maybe he will listen to you."

The girl shrugged with a completely uncaring look on her face. "He doesn't listen to me."

"Try and talk to him," the air hostess insisted.

"He does not like to put seat belts on, I can't make him."

"It is not safe! He has to have the seatbelt on for take-off," the air hostess argued.

"If he doesn't want to, he doesn't want to. I can't make him," the girl snapped and put on her headphones.

The air hostess threw up her hands, huffed and walked away. The little boy kept doing whatever he wanted for the whole trip. He threw his toys all over the place and spread his meal all over himself, the seats around him, the floor, and his exhausted looking nanny. Oh, and he slapped his nanny a few more times.

When we finally landed in Jordan, I breathed a sigh of relief and practically ran off the plane. Even the six hour wait for our connection flight was more appealing than sitting next to that boy.

THE AIRPORT in Amman was quite possibly the smallest in the world with hardly any signs indicating where to go. It took a while but we eventually managed to find the waiting area where we were destined to spend the next six hours of our lives. There were plenty of shops to look at though - Swarovski crystals, elaborate costume jewellery, designer perfume, gold (of course) and a Middle Eastern twist on toys for little girls; dolls dressed in Bedouin costumes and Barbies wearing a burqa. Once we had walked past the same Bedouin dolls and Falafel café for the fifth time I realised, much to my embarrassment, that the airport waiting area was circular. No wonder the sales assistants had stared at us as we walked past them over and over.

A few more laps around the airport and I started to feel hungry. There was a total of three cafés to choose from, so we randomly picked one and bought a couple of bottles of orange juice. After a few acidic sips of what was supposed to be 'fresh' orange juice, resulting in an increasing feeling of nausea, we gave up and relocated to another café that specialized in falafels.

Falafels in a wrap. Falafels in a basket with chips. Falafels with salad or hummus dip.

Like their colleagues in the previous café`, the chef and waiter behind the register were busy chatting. We stood, waiting to order for several minutes before they looked in our direction. As soon as the order was given, they waved us towards a table and promptly resumed whatever they were discussing.

The food didn't take long to arrive, but the order was incomplete.

"Excuse me, where are the drinks?" I asked the waiter before he could leave.

He pointed to the fridge on the back wall. Baffled, I looked back and forth between the waiter and the fridge.

"Um, can I get it myself?"

"What you think? Coke going walk to you?" He laughed heartily at his own joke.

"Oh, yeah, ha ha ha …" I chuckled awkwardly and stood.

Still laughing, the waiter motioned for us to sit and went to get the drinks. With a cheeky smile, he opened them and put in a straw.

"Happy now?" he asked and went back to his chef friend.

Emily and I looked at each other and started to laugh. As tired as I was, I was in a good mood because the food smelt good and we were so close to reaching our destination.

The café grew by another two customers - a French man in a bright floral shirt and several necklaces, and a pretty French woman. It was now their turn to be ignored by the waiter and chef, but they did not find it amusing. When he was not waving his arms around furiously to attract the waiter's attention, the French man complained loudly to his girlfriend. We finished and left while the chef and waiter were still ignoring their new customers.

Finally, it was time to check in for the connecting flight. After being frisked, again, we sat next to a young Palestinian couple, Rita and Jack, from Sydney. Excited to have run into fellow Australians so far away from home, we began to compare our experiences so far in the Middle East. Rita and Jack had also been surprised by the customer service, which is so different to customer service in Australia.

When we eventually boarded, the plane was the smallest I had ever seen. There was room for a maximum of 30 passengers, including the pilot and two flight attendants. Jack and Rita were on the plane, as well as the French man and his girlfriend.

I wonder if they managed to place an order at the café?

"Welcome," the captain's voice greeted us through the microphone system. Although, he could have just spoken and we would have heard him anyway, that's how small the plane was. "Please watch the air hostess as she indicates the emergency exits."

The little boy sitting in front of me tugged on his mother's burqa until she pulled out an iPad and turned it on for him. The air hostess finished her demonstration and sat down.

"Ladies and gentlemen, we are about to take off," the captain announced. "Please turn off all electronic devices because they can interfere with take-off and landing." He repeated his announcement in Arabic.

The little boy's mother made no move to turn off the iPad.

The plane began to move, and the little boy continued playing. My anxiety levels rose.

"Excuse me," I said to the woman. "The captain asked that all electronic devices be turned off. Please turn off your son's iPad."

"He doesn't listen to me," she replied, shrugging her shoulders.

I stared in disbelief. I could understand the little boy resenting his nanny telling him what to do, but this woman was clearly the mother. Before I could come up with a response, two children decided to run down the aisle while the plane was practically vertical in the air.

Panic erupted. The French and Palestinian couples grabbed the little boy and girl to stop them falling over and rolling down the aisle.

"Oh my god!" Emily gasped. "Are they ok??"

"They're ok," Jack answered, holding onto the little boy.

The plane was starting to come out of its vertical position.

"Whose kids are they?" I asked the passengers around me.

Everyone was shaking their heads and looking around for the parents, but no one claimed them. When the plane was horizontal again, the couples released the children and they ran straight to the woman in front of me.

The mother did not seem to share the concern felt by the other passengers, and continued to sit quite calmly in her seat without commenting. Rita and Jack stared with mouths hanging open. The French couple were having a very rapid conversation in French, unimpressed by the recent events if their facial expressions were anything to go by. Emily and I looked at each other in complete disbelief. It took a few minutes for the commotion to die down and by then, we were ready to start descending. We hadn't even risen above the clouds and the poor flight attendant had just managed to finish offering juice boxes to the passengers, when she had to run back to her seat for the landing. I was half amused and half irritated by the incident, but more than anything I was growing impatient to arrive in Israel.

"I don't know about you," I said to Emily, "but all I care about at this point is getting to the hotel and sleeping for at least ten hours! I've had enough of airports."

I had spoken too soon.

CHAPTER 2
A LASTING FIRST IMPRESSION

W e disembarked and lined up to have our passports checked.

"Do you think they'll stamp our passports?" Emily asked.

"Probably," I said cheerfully.

It's five now, and it takes an hour to get to Jerusalem so we can have dinner on the hotel's rooftop! Dinner with a view - What a great start to our holiday!

"What if they don't let us into Jordan because we've been to Israel?"

"Hmm?" I snapped out of my daydream. "Um, the online travel blogs I read recommended asking for a loose leaf visa. We shouldn't have trouble entering Jordan then."

"Oh yeah, I forgot about that. Good idea."

The passport officer in the little booth waved me over.

"Hello," I said cheerfully and gave him my passport.

Barely looking at me, he ignored my greeting and flicked through my passport. He got to the end and started again from the beginning of the little book. After doing that another time, he looked at me with hard eyes.

"What is the purpose of your visit?" he demanded.

"Holiday." I placed my tour itinerary in front of him.

He picked it up and flicked through, then went back to my passport.

Emily edged closer behind me and whispered, "What's taking so long?"

The man heard her and looked up.

"Are you travelling together?" he asked Emily in a more polite tone.

"Yes, we are," Emily told him and handed over her passport and tour documents.

The man looked at Emily's passport and then at mine, both of which were Australian. He asked for my father's name and then my paternal grandfather's name.

Surprised and a little confused by the question, I answered and waited for him to do what he needed to so we could leave. He kept looking at my documents.

"Excuse me," I said, but he didn't look up. "I need a loose leaf visa."

His eyes shot up. He stared at me, his eyebrows scrunched together and his mouth in a hard line.

"What?" he demanded.

What's wrong with him? Why is he so angry?

"I need a loose leaf visa," I repeated.

He returned Emily's passport, but kept mine and made a phone call. I waited silently while he spoke in Hebrew, hung up the phone and continued looking through my documents. There was nothing suspicious about them because I did not have a criminal record and the only other place I had travelled to was Italy.

My stomach knotted. This was weird. Why was he ignoring me? Why did he make a phone call? Why did he give Emily back her travel documents but hold onto mine? And why was he more polite to Emily? I had been friendly and polite to him but he talked to me like I had done something wrong.

Don't jump to conclusions, I told myself. *There must be a perfectly reasonable explanation.*

"Excuse me, is there a problem?"

"Yes," he answered flatly.

My heart rate shot up.

"What's the problem?" I asked, trying hard not to sound nervous.

"Go to room and wait," he ordered, pointing to a corner at the back.

"But – but - what's the problem?" I repeated.

"Go to room!" he snapped.

A few heads turned to look at us.

He kept my passport.

No explanations, no further instructions.

What's happening? Am I in trouble? Why won't he tell me what's wrong? Why won't he give my passport back?

I looked at Emily who seemed just as confused as I felt.

The consulate will know what to do, I thought. *They will be able to explain what is happening.*

"I would like to speak to the Australian consulate," I told the man in what I hoped was a confident and firm.

The next thing that happened shocked and completely terrified me.

"GO TO ROOM!" he shouted, spit flying out of his mouth.

My muscles tensed as he leaned forward and shouted in my face.

"NOW! I TELL YOU GO!"

Not sure where this room was, I looked in the direction he was pointing as he continued to shout. Heart beating hard against my ribcage, I left the queue. Part of me wanted to demand an explanation for his bizarre and aggressive behaviour, but Emily was telling me not to make it worse and just go to the room. I went to the room, uncomfortably aware that he had held onto my passport. I couldn't help remembering the stories in the news about Mossad agents copying passport information and using other people's identities. I tried to tell myself not to be silly and paranoid but in Australia and Europe, you're informed of you rights and given an explanation. I had never experienced anything like this before and it was freaking me out.

The room was small and full of people. White walls, uncomfortable blue plastic chairs, a vending machine and bare, thick, white cement walls. There was no door and an Israeli airport officer stood close to the doorframe listening to people's conversations. He didn't even try to be discreet, but made every effort to make you aware you were being watched.

"Hey, look who's here!" Emily pointed to Rita and Jack.

"What are you two doing here?" Jack and I asked at the same time.

"I got sent here by a grumpy officer who wouldn't tell me why," I complained.

"Ah," Jack said in a knowing tone. "It's because you have an Arabic name."

"What?! No way, that's ridiculous!"

Rita shook her head. "Look around you. Who do you see in this room?"

I looked around the room slowly.

"They do this to me every time I visit," Jack informed me. "It's because I'm Palestinian. Just like everyone else in this room."

I couldn't deny that the room was full of men speaking in Arabic and most women wore a hijab. Other than Emily and I, there were only two other foreigners - a French man talking loudly on his mobile and an American girl with a very strong southern accent.

"But, me and Emily are not Palestinian …"

"Doesn't matter. You have an Arabic name," Jack told me.

"My surname is European," I pointed out.

"Doesn't matter. You have an Arabic first name."

"What does that have to do with anything?" I asked, baffled. "I'm Australian! I mean, I was born in Lebanon but I'm not a citizen there and I have Australian citizenship."

"You were born in Lebanon? That's definitely part of it then."

"But – that's ridiculous, I can't help where I was born! There has to be another reason."

You don't have to believe me," Jack said while Rita examined her manicured nails.

Feeling helpless, I sat down to wait.

I waited, and waited and waited some more. Rita and Jack were called by an officer and didn't come back. Emily was not allowed to stay in the room with me so she hovered by the entrance looking anxious. Boredom did not dull my anxiety, and chatting to the other people being detained added anger to my emotional cocktail. Story after story was about long waiting periods, which they believed was because of their Palestinian identity. I was a little sceptical.

Surely that can't be true? In any case, even if it is true, it doesn't apply to me, I thought.

"But I'm not Palestinian, I'm Australian," I would point out.

They would shake their heads firmly and look at me with pity like one does to a child who insists Santa Clause is real.

"You have Arabic name and born in Lebanon," they told me over and over. Those damning facts, according to them, were the cause for my current misfortune.

It made my blood boil. I had never before been so openly discriminated against or racially stereotyped, and if what the other people were saying was true … well, it was outrageous!

A short, chubby officer with a shiny bald head walked into the room and stared at everyone.

"Excuse me," I called out and walked up to him. "I've been waiting here for over an hour and no one has come to talk to me or explain anything. How much longer will I have to wait?"

"Someone will talk to you soon," he said dismissively, his beady eyes sweeping the room.

Sighing, I returned to my seat and waited some more. No

one came to talk to me so when the same bald officer returned, I walked up to him determined to get answers.

"Excuse me, no one has come to explain what is happening. Why am I being detained like this with no explanation?"

"It is just a random security check, nothing to worry about," he said with a forced smile.

I raised my eyebrows. "That's not what the officer who confiscated my passport said. He told me there was a problem but didn't say what it was."

"It was not his job to explain things to you. I am telling you now there is nothing to worry about and it is a random security check," he said condescendingly.

"Random security check?"

"Yes."

"Why me and not my friend?"

"Maybe because you wear glasses."

Because I wear glasses?! Does he seriously think I am that stupid?

My heart started thudding and heat flooded my cheeks.

"A random security check because I wear glasses?"

"Yes."

"That's a bullshit answer!" I snapped. "It's because my name is Noor and I was born in Lebanon, isn't it?"

"That's a bullshit question! What do you want me to say? That it's true?" he asked, a little too defensively.

"I want the truth!" I told him indignantly. "What's really going on? What's the problem?"

"I told you it's a random security check. Someone will come to talk to you soon. I can see that you are angry so I will let you calm down and come back later."

"Of course I'm angry! This is ridiculous! How come my friend's passport wasn't confiscated but mine was? I'll tell you why, because I have an Arabic name and she doesn't. Random security check – yeah right! This is discrimination! I'm calling the Australian Embassy!"

He was no longer listening, but walking away and keen to

distance himself from the slightly hysterical woman I had become.

I flushed, scared about my predicament and ashamed for losing my temper. I borrowed Emily's mobile to call the Australian embassy for advice but no one picked up. I gave up and sat in the hard chairs to wait some more. An hour later I was taken to another room where an officer sat behind a large desk shuffling some papers.

"You have strange name," he said in a mild manner.

"Yes, it's because I was born in Lebanon and my Italian father chose my name because he thought it was exotic."

I made a mental note to thank him for his choice when I returned to Australia. That is, if I returned and wasn't thrown in an Israeli prison never to be seen or heard from again. Slightly melodramatic, but thirty six hours without sleep does not promote rational and calm thinking.

"Born in Lebanon?" He seemed surprised to learn this, which surprised me.

"It's written on my passport," I pointed out.

"Oh, I have not seen your passport."

My eyebrows shot up. If the papers he was shuffling weren't mine, what was this interview about? What was he reading?

"Is this your first time in Israel?"

"Yes, I'm booked on a tour."

"Where will you go?"

I pulled out my tour itinerary and showed him.

"What is your father and grandfather's name?"

I told him and silently wondered about their obsession with my dad's and grandpa's names.

"Do you know how much longer I might have to wait? Your colleague couldn't tell me, and someone still has my passport. I've been waiting for hours and I'm exhausted …"

He nodded sympathetically. "I can see you look tired. Long flight and waiting, I will try not to keep you waiting too much longer."

"Really?! Oh, thank you so much! I 'm exhausted, I haven't slept in over a day …" I babbled.

"Not much longer now," he ended the interview with a kind smile which I reciprocated.

FEELING MORE HOPEFUL, I walked back to the doorless room. The French man and Southern American girl were still there but most of the other people had been released. Trying to distract myself, I started chatting to them and we exchanged our experiences. The French man imported and exported medical equipment from Lebanon and had an Israeli business partner. He travelled to Israel on a regular basis and was held for hours and questioned about his activities *every single time*. He advised me to just go along with their requests, otherwise they would just keep me waiting. The Southern American girl, Belle, had made an unfortunate mistake. She was returning to the U.S.A after studying Arabic in Jordan for two years and was waiting for her transit flight from Tel Aviv airport. Unfortunately, the Israeli officers could not seem to understand Belle's thick southern accent when she spoke English (I was having a little trouble understanding it too) so she had asked them if they understood Arabic. That was enough to land her in the doorless room. With us was another young American woman of Palestinian origin, Kelly. A petite young woman who covered her hair with a hijab, Kelly was visiting Israel for her sister's wedding. She looked as suspicious as Belle and I did.

The room kept emptying. The French man was called in to be questioned and then was free to go. Belle and Kelly were next, and I was still waiting. Having given up trying to get comfortable on the hard plastic chairs, I sat just outside the doorless room with my back against the wall and my legs stretched out in front of me. It wouldn't hurt to give them a visual reminder that I was still there, in case they had forgotten about me.

Stressed, tired, thirsty and hungry, I watched as the airport gradually emptied. A bunch of passport officers stood in front of the doorless room chatting to each other, drinking coffee, hugging and sharing grapes.

Emily sat next to me on the floor. The airport officers were now completely ignoring us and didn't seem to care if Emily came into the room or not.

"Don't worry, everything will be ok," she repeated for what seemed like the tenth time.

While I appreciated the sentiment, it didn't help soothe my fears. I really couldn't see how she could possibly make that assurance.

"I'm sorry you've been dragged into this," I told her. "You should go. Wait for me outside the airport and if I don't emerge in a few hours, go to the Australian embassy and tell them what happened."

"No way! I've already told you that I am *not* leaving you here alone!"

I felt a rush of gratitude. If anything did happen to me, at least there would be one person who would know about my last hours. Terribly macabre, I know, but I did not have any more internal resources to be optimistic. The fatigue from travel and the stress of the situation, particularly the long wait with no explanation, was making me feel dizzy and nauseous.

"Have some more water. You're still very pale," Emily said at regular intervals.

Belle and Kelly returned from their interviews and sat next to us.

"Are you ok Noor?" Kelly asked. "You don't look so good."

"Tell them if you are not feeling well," Belle advised. "Ask to see a doctor."

My nausea had intensified and I was afraid I would vomit on the floor. To top it all off, my body was shaking uncontrollably. I knew what was happening. This was a bad sign that my body was not coping, even after having taken extra doses of the medication like I was supposed to when my body was under stress. If I didn't improve soon, I would need to have my emergency injection.

By now it was evening and most of the airport officers had left. The four of us were the only passengers left in the airport, and we were all sitting just outside the doorless room with our backs to the wall. We spoke about our lives and compared Australian and American culture. We tried to make jokes and laugh which didn't impress one of the female officers walking past.

She stopped and glared at us. "Are you all travelling together?"

"No, we're waiting," Belle answered.

"Keep waiting," she snapped and walked off.

A little shocked by the unnecessary aggression in her voice, the four of us fell silent as the reality of our situation sank in once again. By this point I was close to tears. I took some more medication but the shaking didn't lessen. My body was going into shock. If I wasn't careful, I could lose consciousness and become seriously ill.

"Excuse me," I called out to one of the officers walking past. "Is there a doctor in the airport? I feel very sick."

"I will check."

Almost half an hour later he still had not returned.

The rude female officer from earlier came and called me. She gave me the option of waiting for the doctor or they could interview me now.

Grasping at the chance of making progress, I said I would start the interview while waiting for the doctor. If this interview was like the previous one, it would be over in a couple of minutes. I had taken enough medication to hopefully avoid an Addisonian crisis, but a doctor's check-up was still needed.

This time I was taken to a different room with three officers, one of which was the rude female officer who seemed to be permanently angry. The other two were men. They spoke Hebrew to each other and didn't bother to translate. When they eventually remembered me, they fired question after question. What was my father and his father's name, my mother's name, when was the last time I had travelled to Lebanon? Did I know anyone in Lebanon? Did I know anyone in Israel? Was I travelling alone? Why was I here? Why was I four days early before my tour?

I pulled out all my travel documents and handed them over. They ignored me for a few minutes and spoke to each other in Hebrew.

My muscles shook and my stomach heaved.

"I really need to see the doctor," I told them feebly.

Stupid, I chided myself. *I should have asked to see him before this interview.*

"Doctor is busy. There is only one doctor in the airport and he has other people to see," officer one said.

"Maybe he go home already," officer two shrugged.

They continued with the questions. What did I do for a living? Did I have a boyfriend? Was I meeting someone here? Why didn't I have a boyfriend? Did I have a mobile phone? No? Why not? Emily had one, so I didn't bring mine. They seemed very surprised that I was not married and kept coming back to the topic.

"I'm only 24!" I said incredulously.

"So what? 24 is old enough to be married. Many people marry at 24."

"Not in Melbourne," I told them, resentful of the intrusion into my non-existent love life.

"You are planning on meeting anyone here?" officer one asked with a smirk.

I frowned.

"No," I said very coldly and firmly.

I understood what he was implying and I did not appreciate it. I hated the reputation that western women seem to have when travelling, as though we are ready to jump into bed with anyone who says hello.

"Really? You don't know anyone here? You are not meeting someone?"

"No, I am not. I've never been here before, so how could I know anyone?"

More Hebrew conversation between the three of them, without bothering to translate for me. They kept looking through my guide book and laughing at my colour coded itinerary.

I watched them without saying anything for a while, but I wasn't feeling better so I asked for the doctor again. I showed them my medic alert bracelet and explained that I had a chronic illness. They recognised the medic alert symbol, but did not seem very concerned. I insisted that they either page the doctor or call an ambulance, either one would do. This seemed to catch their attention and after saying they would try to find him, they dismissed me back to the doorless room. Instead, I headed straight for the bathroom around the corner and leaned over the sink until the urge to vomit passed. Taking deep breaths, I splashed water on my face and neck with shaking hands.

When I returned to the doorless room, I found a very worried Emily, a grey haired man carrying a medical bag, and his younger assistant.

"What happened? Where did you go?" Emily asked.

"Sorry, I thought I was going to be sick so I went to the bathroom."

Emily turned to the doctor and explained what had happened.

Shaking his head in disbelief, he sent his assistant to fetch my passport and started to examine me.

My legs were shaking and without wasting any more time, I pulled out my injection kit.

"I have Addison's disease and need to have my emergency injection. I took 100mg in tablets over an hour ago but I didn't get better at all."

Nodding knowingly, he opened his black bag and quickly pulled on gloves.

I had practiced administering the injection on oranges at home, in case I ever needed it in an emergency, but after accidentally breaking the needle in an orange, I didn't fancy my chances of doing it successfully now. Especially not when my hands were trembling so much. Hoping to avoid embarrassment, I presented him with my arm.

"Ahem," the doctor cleared his throat, blushing. "I need to inject a fleshy area to avoid bruising and muscle pain ..." he explained apologetically. "Your, um - bottom is better choice."

Cringing, I nodded in resignation. I knew it was the correct area for the injection, but I had been hoping to avoid any further public mortification. There was nowhere else to go and there was no door for privacy.

He looked as awkward and embarrassed as I felt. Shaking my head in disbelief at my luck, I started laughing, turned around and pulled down my leggings to reveal part of my bottom.

Emily stared in shock for a second and quickly looked away to give me some non-existent privacy. A loud gasp from the corner drew my eyes to a Muslim couple who scurried out of the room, throwing shocked looks over their shoulders. I hadn't even noticed them before. They must have arrived while I was being questioned.

Please hurry up! I silently pleaded as the doctor carefully prepared the injection.

I heard another gasp. My head turned towards the entrance where a young female airport officer was staring with her mouth hanging open.

Now do you believe me? I thought to myself, half amused at her facial expression and half angry that it had taken so long for me to receive medical care.

I couldn't tell who was most embarrassed - me with part

of my bottom on show, Emily who was determinately looking at the ceiling, the blushing doctor, the Muslim couple who had escaped or the officer who could not seem to close her mouth.

The doctor's assistant returned with my passport and entry visa just as I pulled up my leggings. I thanked the doctor repeatedly and collapsed in a chair, sobbing with relief and exhaustion. Emily patted my back for several minutes while I tried to compose myself. The doctor's kindness and concern had moved me. He had treated me with respect, which was a stark difference to the brusque treatment I had received from his colleagues.

"Let's get out of here," I sniffed to Emily and ran out of the horrible doorless room towards the luggage collection area.

Part of me wanted to get back on a plane and return straight home to Melbourne, but my immediate priority was to get out of the airport before those airport officers changed their minds. We waited for our luggage to appear on the carousel, gave up and searched through the lost luggage pile. No sign of our suitcases. Fortune was finally smiling on me because I spotted an airport officer and asked him for help. He asked for our names and we handed him our passports.

"Where have you been?" he burst out. "Your plane landed three hours ago! I was just putting your luggage in storage because you didn't collect it. I thought you missed your flight!"

Emily, still indignant and worried on my behalf, told him that his colleagues had kept me for over three hours.

Shaking his head, he sighed and said sarcastically, "Welcome to Israel."

I burst out laughing - a high pitched, strained and slightly hysterical laugh.

CHAPTER 3
A MEMORABLE ENTRANCE

At some point in between the airport exit and taxi pickup area, I started sobbing again. I wasn't even aware of it until a young man with an Israeli accent asked me if I was alright. Sniffling, I mumbled something even I didn't understand and looked for a Nesher taxi. According to my trusty travel guidebook, it was much cheaper than a regular taxi because you had to share with other passengers. The disadvantage of a shared taxi is that most don't leave until they are full of passengers, and the trip can take longer depending on everyone's destination. Maybe my luck was turning because I found one that was almost ready to go just outside the entrance. It was a sort of white minivan that was already half full of people, complete with a loud and flustered driver trying to get as many passengers as possible.

Emily kept throwing me concerned looks but I was ignoring them, trying hard to supress the sobbing I couldn't seem to stop.

"Excuse me, how much is it to Jerusalem?" Emily asked the driver while I drew deep breaths and tried to compose myself.

"60 shekel each."

Emily looked at me and I started to nod, but before I could

finish nodding the driver had grabbed our luggage and thrown it unceremoniously into the boot.

"Sit, sit," he ushered us urgently.

Our travelling companions were a young couple with a baby, three young American girls, an American woman and an elderly orthodox Jewish man. While the other passengers chatted, I alternated between crying and swearing while Emily patted my back sympathetically. It took a few minutes, but I finally managed to get myself under control.

"Why are we still waiting?" someone asked from the back seat.

The driver broke off his debate with the older orthodox Jewish man to announce in English,

"He cannot sit next to woman, we need change seats."

Besides the young couple with the baby, all the passengers were female so the couple were forced to separate. I stared in disbelief as the young mother, with much grace and dignity, quietly moved to the back of the taxi with the baby to join the rest of us women. I wondered what would have happened if the young couple had refused to separate. Would we have all been stuck waiting at the airport hoping another man joined our jolly crew? Or would the religious man have disembarked and found alternative transport? So far on this trip, my name, ethnicity and now gender had proven to be problematic. All I needed was for my religion to be included and I would have the complete experience!

"What do you want to do?" Emily asked as the driver closed the boot and got into the van. "If you want to go back home, we can leave immediately."

Tempting, oh so tempting … and I was upset and angry enough to go through with it.

"I just want to get away from this airport," I told her in a croaky voice.

"Ok, how about this? We'll go to the hotel and get some sleep, then decide tomorrow morning when we are both calmer and rested," she suggested.

I nodded and wiped my eyes with a tissue. She was right. I was sleep deprived and in shock. It was not a good time to make decisions.

THE NESHER TAXI dropped several people off at various points when it reached Jerusalem, so we were some of the last people on board.

"You," the driver pointed to us, "where you go?"

I showed him the address of the hotel we had booked.

"Is in Old City. Car no go in," the driver shook his head, his longish shaggy grey hair fluttering around his chubby face. "I drop you here, you walk."

"What?!" I gasped in alarm. "But … but it's dark! How will we find the hotel?"

"Cars no fit, street too small," he shook his head again. "I drop you Damascus Gate. Short walk, easy."

"Where is the Damascus Gate?" I asked looking around for a street sign.

"Down there," he pointed into the blackness of the night.

Without waiting for a response, he promptly got out, unloaded our suitcases and held out his hand for the fare.

"I have no change," he told us with his fist tightly clenched around the large notes.

"Fine," I said through gritted teeth.

He had given himself a very sizeable tip, and we had to walk the rest of the way. This night just kept getting better and better.

With the money in his hand, he jumped back in and drove off without looking back.

So there we were on the sidewalk of a road in, presumably, Jerusalem. The street was wide and seemed to be divided in the middle by a tunnel which cars sped through, but the part where we were was deserted.

"He said it wasn't far, and easy to find …" Emily tried sounding optimistic.

I sighed and started pulling my suitcase behind me. "At least it's downhill."

We walked and walked, eyes straining in the dim street lights, searching for the Damascus Gate but the wall seemed to continue seamlessly and endlessly.

"I can't see any signs, or the Damascus entrance," Emily said in a worried tone. "I hope we are going in the right direction."

A tall figure in a long black coat, large hat and with swinging dreadlocks was moving closer to us from the opposite direction.

"I'll ask him for directions," I told her.

A religiously observant person is unlikely to hurt us, I told myself to quell my nerves. *I hope.*

"Excuse me," I called out loudly, while my hand automatically tightened around the strap of the hand luggage, just in case I needed to swing it as a weapon.

He was close enough now that I could see his eyes dart to me and then just as quickly to the empty road.

"Can you help us? We're looking for the Damascus Gate."

No answer. He averted his eyes and walked faster, leaving us to stare at his back.

I turned to Emily with raised eyebrows. "He saw us, right?"

"Maybe he doesn't know English," she answered with a shrug.

With no one else in sight to ask for directions, we had no alternative but to keep walking and hoping we would eventually stumble upon the gate. With no sign of the Damascus Gate, doubt got the better of us and we retraced our steps to our drop off point hoping to ask someone for directions.

"Look!" Emily pointed to a white van parked on the side of the road where the taxi driver had dropped us off.

"He came back for us!"

I ran uphill, dragging my suitcase behind me and desperately hoping he wouldn't leave without us. My legs strained but I pushed on until I was close enough to see the driver and came to an abrupt halt. That was not our taxi driver. Instead, a young and middle aged man were staring at me in astonishment from inside the van.

I was crushed. Clearly, the taxi driver's conscience had not made him come back for us.

What do I do now?

I was torn between asking them for directions and nervous of approaching two strange men in a van. The headline *'Young tourist missing on her first night in Jerusalem'* flashed through my mind. Keeping my distance from the van, just in case I needed to make a run for it, I asked where the Damascus Gate was. Thankfully, the men spoke English and assured me that if I followed the wall all the way down the hill I would reach the elusive entrance to the Old City of Jerusalem. It seemed Emily and I had given up too soon and retraced our steps when we should have walked on. Not wanting to give them the opportunity to offer us a lift, I thanked them and briskly walked away. I felt guilty assuming the worst of these men, but better safe than sorry. I led the way back down the hill, this time determined to keep following the wall no matter how long it took.

Wall, more wall and finally, there it was! The biggest doorway I had ever seen - high enough to fit a man mounted on a horse and wide enough for several people side by side. Some people were still walking around and there were even a few street vendors just in front of the entrance. Most of the light seemed to be coming from inside the gate entrance, leaving the courtyard in front dimly illuminated.

A row of taxi drivers sitting on a bench and smoking, watched our progress with interest. As soon as we were within earshot, they started vying for our attention, each assuring us that he was the one we needed, he was the one who could take us anywhere we wanted for less.

I frowned. "I thought the nesher driver said no cars could fit in the streets of the Old City?"

Emily nodded. "These guys seem convinced they can drive into the Old City though," she said uncertainly. "What do you think? Is it worth it?"

"I don't know," I said, putting down my backpack. "I mean, we're finally at the gate but how far is the hotel from here?"

"Yeah, I was wondering about that too. What if it's another long walk? It's already 9.30 pm, and we don't really know where we're going. We could ask how much," Emily suggested.

I nodded and went over to them. After telling the drivers the name of our hotel, being assured that each knew where it was located and that it was still another fifteen minute walk, and it was better to catch his taxi, I was almost convinced until one of them told me it was fifty shekels. We chose to walk.

It took a while but we managed to get our luggage down the many steps more or less in one piece. Pushing my hair back from my face, I grinned and high fived Emily.

"Why you no use ramp?"

I turned to see an old man shuffling past. He lifted his walking stick and pointed it to the right side of the gate entrance.

Barely visible in the darkness was a large and wonderful ramp.

My shoulders slumped. "We didn't see it," I mumbled and the old man chuckled.

"Never mind," said Emily. "Hopefully the hotel is close by."

A young boy materialised out of the darkness. "Where you go? I take you, only 20 shekels," he said, jumping around us like an energetic grasshopper.

"No thank you, we know where we're going," I lied.

"Good deal. 20 shekels," he insisted and held out his hand. "I know all hotels."

"No, thank you," Emily smiled at him, but he would not be discouraged.

Trying to ignore the energetic boy still bouncing around us, we passed through the gate and into the deserted Old City. We walked until we reached a junction in the road, where it suddenly split into two narrow lanes. Both were equally dark and empty.

"Come on, 20 shekels!"

The old man had slowly caught up. Waving his stick at the young boy, he told him off in Arabic. "Leave them alone! I will show them the way."

I shamelessly eavesdropped to their conversation in Arabic. The young boy tried convincing the old man to let him take us to the hotel and promised to share the money. The old man waved his stick at him again and told him to buzz off. Grumbling, the young boy gave up and left.

"What is name hotel?" the old man asked us.

I told him and he pointed to the right lane with his walking stick.

"Go there. Walk, walk, walk until see hotel."

"Thank you so much! Thank you!" Emily and I babbled.

The old man smiled and nodded farewell. I watched him walk away, a little lost for words. He had stopped others from taking advantage of our ignorance and helped us find our way without asking for anything in return. What a kind soul!

"Thank goodness we ran into him," Emily said after he had walked off.

"I know! We would have been so lost without his help." I eyed the very long and dimly lit lane. "Well, at least we can't take a wrong turn."

"Look, a bakery is still open!" Emily pointed to a tiny shop at the corner of the junction. "We should get some food in case the hotel restaurant is already closed."

"Hello," I waved to the man packing up the goods on display. "Can we buy?"

He nodded and waved us over. The selection was limited

but we walked away with a stack of oval bread rings covered with sesame seeds.

We walked, and walked and walked. We passed a sign for a hostel, worried we had gone too far, but decided not to repeat the Damascus Gate fiasco and kept walking. Two young men stopped their conversation to watch us drag our suitcases past them as fast as we could. Another young man came to a complete standstill and stared while we scurried along.

It's almost 10, I thought uneasily. *Shouldn't we have found it by now? All I see is closed shops.*

"I think I see it!" Emily said quietly, trying not to wake the locals.

When I saw what she was pointing at my heart sank a little. The small sign and door made it look more like the entrance to one of the local houses, not a hotel like it was advertised. I pushed the door open and gasped. The longest and steepest staircase I have ever seen took up my entire field of vision.

"I hope there's an elevator ..." Emily said with wide eyes.

"No elevator. I help," a kind sounding voice said from my right.

A petite, young Japanese woman bowed. "Hello. I am Akari. I stay here, I help carry," she said, pointing to our suitcases.

"Thank you but they are heavy - "

She shook her head, smiled and lifted my suitcase all the way up to the foyer, while I clumsily helped Emily with hers. While I sweated and swore with the effort, Akari calmly and elegantly managed my suitcase as though her slim figure hid muscles of steel.

"Arigato gozaimas," I thanked her in the little Japanese I could remember from high school.

With a big smile, she bowed and continued up the staircase to where I assumed the guest bedrooms were.

I turned to find the hotel concierge staring in astonishment.

"Hello, we're checking in," I said.

"It's after 10 pm. Check in closed," he answered, adjusting the white cap on his head.

"Oh, sorry, um … Ahmed, " I said, squinting at the name tag. "I should have explained. We have a booking."

"We booked for four days," Emily told him.

Ahmed stroked his long and bushy beard while he read the papers I had given him.

"I am sorry, there is error with booking. We not expect you until tomorrow night."

"What?! But that's impossible!" I had made the booking and double checked the dates.

Oh no … Did I forget about the time difference and book the wrong day? Well, that would be the cherry on top of my large bad luck cake!

"I am so sorry, your room not ready. We expect you tomorrow. Come back tomorrow. So sorry," he said looking at us with concern.

On the verge of tears, again, I kept looking from Ahmed to Emily with my mouth opening and closing like a fish.

"But …but …where will we go?" I asked pitifully.

What other hotel will we find at this hour? We're going to have to sleep on the street!

"Why you so late?" Ahmed demanded. "It is past ten pm, too late to check in!"

"Actually, we arrived at five in the afternoon but got held up at the airport. We've just arrived to Jerusalem now," Emily explained.

"Why keep you at airport so long?" Ahmed asked curiously.

"Because I have an Arabic name!" I exploded, surprising myself, Emily and the concierge.

It seems I haven't quite forgiven those airport officers for all the trouble they caused me, I thought.

Comprehension dawned on Ahmed's face and his lips pressed together in a grim line. Emily recounted our little adventure at the airport while he nodded and stroked his beard.

"Your surname not Arabic. It sounds European," he said, waving the booking with my name on it. "Why you have Arabic name and foreign surname?"

I sighed and, once again, explained that I was the product of two nationalities merging together. Slightly baffled by the local's fascination with my parentage, which I had thought was fairly common, I could only conclude that must not be the case in this part of the world. Parentage seemed to be a very important part of a person's identity here, quite different to Australia where people are more individualistic. In this instance however, my name proved to be an asset rather than a hindrance.

Ahmed began clicking his computer mouse and squinting at the monitor screen. "I have only one free room. Not ready for guests, but you sleep tonight until guests check out of your room tomorrow morning."

Relief flooded my body and I almost started crying.

"Thank you so much!"

"We really appreciate it," Emily added, sounding as relieved as I felt.

"You need anything? I am night concierge and you need something, tell me. I look after you," Ahmed told us.

"Oh, thank you! Where can we buy water bottles from?" Emily asked looking around the hotel lobby for a vending machine.

"Water? No worry," Ahmed waved his hand. "Ibrahim," he called out loudly.

A thin young man materialised in front of Ahmed's desk, nodded his head rapidly while he received instructions and picked up our suitcases.

"Ibrahim take you to room, then get you water," Ahmed told us. "Goodnight."

I accepted our set of keys on a comically large key ring and dragged my feet upstairs to our room. Ibrahim left our suitcases at the door and disappeared down the stairs to get our water, although where he could have gone at this time of night was a mystery.

"You'll feel much better after a shower and a good night's sleep," Emily told me.

"Yea," I mumbled distracted by my first view of the room.

It was …cozy. That's code for small. I wasn't about to complain though. We had a safe place to sleep tonight with a private bathroom and air conditioning. I doubted we would need it because despite the heat during the day, the night was refreshingly cool. Slight problem with the bed, though. One large double bed rather than the twin beds we had requested as part of the booking. Never mind, beggars can't be choosers and I was still very grateful he hadn't turned us away.

"I hope the room we booked is a bit bigger than this one," Emily mused as she took in the space, which appeared even smaller with our suitcases by the bed. "You can have a shower first if you like," Emily generously offered. "I'll start unpacking my things."

"Thanks, I won't be long," I promised and entered the equally cozy bathroom.

I stood under the shower with my face turned upwards, eyes closed with a big smile. I turned the knobs to full blast and waited for the water. My smile faltered but did not disappear, any second now.

Trickle, trickle, trickle.

Not the strong water pressure I had eagerly anticipated, but perhaps it took a while to arrive.

Trickle, trickle.

Eyes open and smile completely gone, I stared at the water dripping down weakly. With a deep and lengthy sigh, I made the best of it before going to break the bad news to Emily, not that it stopped her trying to shower.

While she was gone I looked through the maps in my guide-book. An idea had formed in the back of my mind which, if I was correct, might explain the hostile behaviour of the airport officers. I compared the hotel's location to the map in my book and gasped. It was located in the Muslim quarter of the Old City of Jerusalem. The hotel website did not mention that it was located in the Muslim quarter, I was sure of that.

Is this why they held me for so long? Because they saw my booking in this hotel? I thought with dismay. We had chosen this hotel based on other factors: cost, proximity to sights and the incredible city view from the rooftop terrace. Could my Arabic name and booking in a hotel in the Muslim quarter have rung alarm bells in their heads?

That's their problem! I thought indignantly. *They need to realise that the entire world is not divided based on religious categories, as Jerusalem seems to be!*

According to the map, the Old City of Jerusalem was divided into four quarters - the Jewish quarter, Muslim quarter, Christian quarter and Armenian quarter. It was a completely new concept to me. In Melbourne, there is no 'Muslim' hotel in the 'Muslim quarter' of the city. People just live where they can afford to and someone's religion is seen as private.

A gentle knock on the door distracted me from my theorising. Ibrahim had turned up with several large water bottles which I had forgotten about. I paid him, with a generous tip for troubling him so late at night, and enjoyed the cold water sitting on the edge of the bed. My eyes scanned the room again and took in the out-dated furniture and cracks in the wall and ceiling. I didn't mind though, it gave the room a rather quaint feel.

"Did the water pressure improve?" I asked Emily when she came out of the bathroom.

"No," she answered and picked up a water bottle. "How much do I owe you for the water?"

"Don't worry about it, it's on me. Should we eat this bread now or save it for breakfast?"

"I'm hungry," Emily answered.

"Me too. Look, the baker even gave us zaatar to have with the bread."

"What's that?"

"It's a mix of herbs that you dip the bread in. At home though, mum mixes it with olive oil and spreads it on the bread. You can even bake it like a pizza and eat it with fresh tomatoes and cucumber," I explained excitedly.

"That sounds delicious! It's going to be easy being vegan here."

I started laughing loudly. "Do you realise we are literally having bread and water for dinner, like prisoners?"

Emily laughed. "Yea but this bread is so good. It's so light and fluffy."

It was getting close to midnight and the exhaustion was kicking in with full force.

"Are you feeling better? Did the injection help?" Emily asked.

"Yea, it really helped. I should have done it earlier, but I wasn't thinking straight and my hands were shaking too much," I told her. "Sleep will help. I will feel even better in the morning."

Emily nodded and pulled back the bed covers.

"EEEEEWWWWW!"

"COCKROACH!"

"What?! Where?" Emily demanded.

I pointed to the floor where a big cockroach scuttled across the tiled floor and disappeared behind the TV cabinet.

"Wait, why did you say 'eeew'?" I asked.

Emily pointed to the bed sheets and pillowcases which had questionable stains on them.

"Maybe we should sleep on our beach towels …" I suggested.

"Yes, and use our aeroplane neck pillows instead of these ones," Emily added.

Not ideal, but I was too tired to worry about the stains or my cockroach friend coming back to visit during the night. A small part of me, the part still recovering from shock, was expecting the airport officers to burst into the room and arrest me at any moment.

Don't be silly, I told myself but couldn't quite shake the feeling of unease. Thankfully though, my body was too exhausted to permit nightmares of being chased and interrogated. My eyes closed of their own will and for the first time in my life, I fell asleep immediately. That's how I spent my first day in Israel and Jerusalem. A memorable entry and first night in a memorable city. Quite fitting, actually.

CHAPTER 4
JERUSALEM

I woke as the first rays of light danced on my eyelids. The fear and stress from yesterday seemed like an unpleasant dream, and with the new dawn came the promise of a fresh start. It was still early, only 5 am, but I was far too excited to sleep any more. I lay with my eyes closed for a moment longer, savouring the realisation that I was in Jerusalem. Everything about it so far had been very different to what I was used to in Melbourne, and I was excited to explore this new world. I opened my eyes and looked around the room, half afraid to see more cockroaches but luckily there was no sign of them. The room looked even shabbier in the daylight, but to my surprise I found it charming and full of character. Mind you, my enthusiasm was slightly dampened when I used the dripping shower again, but not by much.

"Sorry, did I wake you?" I asked Emily who was sleepily rubbing her eyes.

"No, you didn't." She yawned and stretched.

"It's still very early, get some more sleep."

"Actually, I'm feeling pretty refreshed. How did you sleep?" she asked.

"I can't believe I slept at all after the cockroach incident last night. I must have been really exhausted!"

"Me too," Emily agreed. "Is the water pressure in the shower better today?"

"Nope. I have to say, this room looks very different to the photos shown on the internet …"

"I know! I hope the next room they put us in is better," said Emily. "I'll have a quick shower and we can start our day of exploring."

Emily didn't take long to get ready and we were out of the hotel before 6am. All the stores were shut and besides us, only a few people were walking down the narrow lane. Even though it was almost deserted like last night, it was all much less intimidating, welcoming even, in the soft light of the morning.

"What's on the itinerary today?" Emily adjusted her backpack.

Like me, her camera was strapped to her wrist so we wouldn't have to search through our bags every time we wanted to take a picture.

"Umm …" I pulled out the colour coded day-by-day itinerary which I had laboured over. "I had written down the Russian compound and Mea Sherim, but I didn't realise they were outside the Old City."

Emily studied the map thoughtfully. "It's not too far, I'm sure we can manage the walk."

"Yeah, but we'll have to walk back to the Old City if we want to do the rampart walk."

"That's ok," Emily smiled. "I don't mind walking."

"Alright, let's go!" I grinned and led the way back to the Damascus Gate.

While I can't read maps, I find my way around by memorizing landmarks and using them as a reference point. Even though I had arrived at night and walked in the dark, I recognised the crossroad we had stopped at and the entrance to the city without much trouble. We walked out of the Damascus Gate, crossed the bridge and stood on the steps we had struggled to drag our suitcases down the previous night.

"Give me a minute," I called out to Emily. "I want to take some pictures of the elusive Damascus Gate. I can't believe how hard it was to find last night …"

The sun was rising higher, illuminating the gate with a golden light. It was spectacular to behold an ancient city waking to a new day.

Emily, who was more skilled with a camera than me, took photos to capture the moment.

"When I read that there is an Old Jerusalem and New Jerusalem, I didn't realise they were so separate," I commented, watching street vendors set up just outside the gate.

"What do you mean?"

"Well, I thought that Old Jerusalem was some ancient buildings among the newer ones of New Jerusalem. Like Rome. I didn't realise that it is a city within a city."

I opened the guide book onto the map of Jerusalem. "According to this, Old Jerusalem is the original city," I read out. "It is enclosed by a thick stone wall that served as a form of defence throughout history, and the only way in or out was through the eight gates. As the population grew and could no longer be accommodated within the wall, the city expanded into the areas around it."

Emily studied the map in the book. "New Jerusalem seems a lot closer on the map."

I nodded then realised she couldn't see me if she was reading. "So, essentially, Jerusalem is one unified city, but in reality there are two parts - Old Jerusalem and New Jerusalem. It's a bit confusing …"

"If we go left and then up Jaffa street, it's the easiest route to get to New Jerusalem, and from there it's not far to where we want to go," Emily traced the route with her fingertip.

"Sounds good to me. Lead on!"

We walked up the same hill we had walked down the night before, which was just as steep as I remembered, but less intimidating in daylight. At one point we had to stop and ask for directions and the only other people around were two young orthodox men. I half expected them to keep walking like the man from last night, but they stopped to help us. They could not speak English and my Hebrew was very basic so we resorted to using a language all humans have in common; body language. Many smiles, laughs, pointing and shoulder shrugs later we were headed in the right direction to the new city of Jerusalem. I stopped at a tiny shop to buy bagels for breakfast and was thrilled when the shopkeeper seemed to understand my Hebrew.

THE FIRST SIGHT-SEEING item on our itinerary was the Russian compound that housed the Holy Trinity Cathedral. It looked lovely in the travel guide pictures, but for some reason when we arrived there were heavily armed police officers standing in front of it.

"Um, my guide book doesn't say anything about guards with guns ..." I whispered, a little alarmed by the stony looks on their faces.

"Maybe this is normal and they always stand at the entrance of the church?"

"Or maybe there's some local tension or incident we don't know about. Let's not stop, we'll just go to Mea Sherim," I suggested.

Emily nodded and after consulting the map, led us to the neighbourhood of Mea Sherim.

"So, why exactly do you want to see this neighbourhood?"

"Curiosity. Remember I told you about my fieldwork at a synagogue for my anthropology thesis?" I didn't pause long enough for Emily to answer. "Well, the Rabbi of the synagogue is an orthodox Jew and he told me that in Mea Sherim, they are even more conservative and orthodox than him! Apparently it is one of the most ultra-orthodox and religiously conservative neighbourhoods in Israel. He thought I'd find it interesting."

"Ok." Emily seemed amused. "If it's so religious, it's a good thing we wore the ankle length skirts. Should we wear our cardigans too?"

"Yeah, probably ..." I pulled on my long sleeve cardigan in resignation. It was already very warm and I hated feeling hot.

It was still very early in the morning, and few people were out on the streets. I walked slowly, enjoying the tranquillity and quietness, stopping frequently to look around. I watched the neighbourhood wake up and slowly come alive; young children being taken to school by their mothers, shop owners opening their stores for the day and the road slowly filling with cars. It was lovely to be part of the neighbourhood as it greeted a new day.

We wandered deeper into Mea Sherim, into a less affluent part of the neighbourhood that had many run-down buildings. Besides me and Emily, there were no other tourists and I did not see any non-religious Israelis either.

I hope they don't find our presence intrusive, I worried. *Or are they used to tourists wandering around and just ignore them?*

The locals in this neighbourhood had exceptional self-control. No one looked at us, not even the small children on their way to school. It was almost like being invisible.

"Oh, look how fresh that fruit looks!" Emily pointed to the crates on display outside of a small green grocer's store.

"I could use something sweet after that very salty bagel!"

"You did well with the bagels," Emily encouraged. "And now you have another opportunity to practice your Hebrew. What do you feel like having?"

"Well, the only fruit I can remember how to say right now is banana which is *bananot*."

I laughed along with Emily.

"That's fine. Probably better than an apple anyway, because we would have to wash it first with our bottled water."

"Shalom," the middle aged, portly, green grocer greeter us as we moved closer.

"Shalom," we responded with a smile.

"Yesh Banannot?" I asked, hoping he could understand my pronunciation.

He gave me a bemused smile adults often give to toddlers who are learning to speak.

"Ken." He pointed inside the store and made a gesture to follow.

"Kamah Zeh Oleh?"

He held up three fingers and I counted out the coins. Emily accepted the bag full of bananas (I may have accidentally bought a kilo) and turned towards the door, but the man wanted to chat. He was curious about where we were from (luckily I had learned how to say 'I am Australian'), how long we had been here, and welcomed us to Israel. Now this was more like the welcome I had imagined! Snack successfully purchased, we waved goodbye to our new friend and headed towards the next destination, the centre of New Jerusalem.

I STARED WITH WIDE EYES. "Wow! It looks so …European!"

Large paved streets, mosaics decorating the walls, statues, chic cafés, tempting ice cream stores, clothing boutiques and hanging flower pots from French style verandas adorning expensive looking apartments. Well-dressed people walked their dogs on leashes, or jogged behind them, while cats with glossy coats stared at them scornfully from their balconies. People walked around with a leisurely pace or congregated to socialise in Italian inspired piazzas (city square). With the green iron benches adorning the sides of streets and a tram line running through the city centre, I felt as though I was back in Melbourne.

"We need to come back here and do some shopping!" Emily announced and I agreed.

The stores had beautiful artisan items on display and I had

a feeling my wallet would become a lot lighter after a shopping trip here.

"Look, Israeli soldiers buying ice-cream!" I giggled like an immature teenager.

It was such a strange image, soldiers armed with guns licking an ice-cream cone.

"They must be on their break. I can't imagine their commanding officer would be too happy about them walking around eating ice-cream while on duty."

I looked at the people walking past, greeting each other and going about their daily business. They seemed very relaxed, and it added to the atmosphere of the place as peaceful and prosperous. I noticed that although many men wore kippahs (cap worn by Jewish men) to signify they were religiously observant, no one wore the distinctive black clothes and large fur hats of the ultra-orthodox tradition, like in Mea-Sherim. I even heard Arabic and saw Jews and non-Jews mingling together.

"Let's come back tomorrow," Emily suggested.

"Yep, sounds good to me."

We headed back towards the Old City where we planned to spend the rest of the day.

"Hey, are those the guys from this morning, the ones who gave us directions?" Emily asked.

I looked in the direction she was pointing and waved back at them. They grinned and waved more enthusiastically as they kept walking.

"I can't believe they managed to understand what I was asking. I felt like a mime."

Their friendly reaction was enough to dispel any unpleasant residue from my experiences the night before. To be recognised and greeted like a friend made me feel welcome and happy to be there. It was going to be a good day.

• • •

A SHORT WALK downhill and we were back at the Old City. This time, we entered through Jaffa Gate which is one of two starting points for a walk around the Old City walls. What a stark contrast! The narrow lanes were packed with vendors selling their wares from tiny shops or street carts, and large crowds of tourists and locals trying to navigate the small spaces.

Emily gasped. "Is that car really going into the lane?!

My jaw dropped as I watched a car slowly make its way down the narrow lane, forcing people to plaster themselves against the walls to avoid being run over.

"But – but - the taxi guy said cars don't fit in the Old City…"

"Apparently that doesn't stop them from trying," Emily answered wryly.

Here in the Old City, chaos reigned. Loud, bustling and vibrant, it made the New City seem like another world far away, when in actual fact it was only a fifteen minute walk.

Hard to believe they are both part of the same city, I thought, utterly fascinated.

"What section of the city are we in?" I peered at the map Emily was studying.

"I think we are on the border of the Christian and Armenian quarters."

I looked around and spotted a sign in English advertising a walk on the ramparts of the Old City walls. "I think we can buy the tickets there."

The ticket booth was a very basic table with a plastic chair, and an older man with a box to collect money. The signs in English suggested that this was a popular tourist activity.

"I bet the view will be amazing. We should be able to see the whole city from the top of the wall," Emily said as she got her camera ready.

"That's if we make it up to the top of the wall. Have you seen these tiny and steep stairs?"

"Should we go back to the hotel and change into our hiking shoes first? And pants?"

I eyed the numerous stairs. "We can if you want to, but I'm fine with my thongs."

"Ok, but lift your skirt off the ground so you don't step on it and trip."

I lifted my long skirt as high as modestly possible and hoped there was no one below looking up. The path to get to the top of the wall was long and narrow with uneven, slippery steps.

"It's a good thing we packed sunglasses and water bottles," Emily said before drinking. "The view is spectacular! Well worth the climb."

"Yes, and I bet it's even more incredible at night. Too bad we didn't bring any flashlights."

"It would be dangerous to do this climb at night," Emily pointed out and I sighed in disappointment, but I knew she was right.

The path was quite narrow in some parts and as spectacular as the views were, it was challenging enough in daylight.

Several other tourists were also walking along the top of the Old City walls, and they would occasionally get caught in a traffic jam in the narrow pathways. It was easy enough for us to avoid getting caught in it too by keeping up a lively pace. Unfortunately, it was not quite as easy to avoid a large group of young American Jewish students following their Israeli tour guide. Up so much higher than the city and its dwellings, we could hear every sound. Unfortunately along with the poetic sounds of the wind whistling through the narrow passageway and birds chirping, I heard the loud and constant Hebrew phone conversation of the Israeli guide. Trying in vain to leave the noisy group behind us, we kept walking faster until the passage narrowed too much and required a slower pace.

"Oh, look at the magnificent view." Emily began snapping

pictures. "You can see the entire city of Jerusalem, old and new!"

I shot an alarmed look behind us. "Hurry up, they're getting closer!"

I could see them now, gangly teenagers flirting with each other as the tour guide ignored them and continued her conversation in Hebrew. Hanging up the phone, which had been glued to her ear until that moment, she pinned me to the spot with her gaze and spoke rapidly in Hebrew.

"Oh, um, sorry I'm not Israeli …" It was a little thrilling to be mistaken for a local.

She switched to English without batting an eyelid. "You, hello! We lost. How get off wall?"

I looked at Emily with raised eyebrows, desperately trying to smother the laughter that threatened to spill out. Of all the ridiculous things in the world! A native Israeli tour guide leading a group of American teenagers, asking for directions from Australian tourists! Unfortunately, it was not her lucky day because we were quite happily lost, and content to just keep walking along the rampart passage until it ended. It seemed more adventurous that way, instead of following map directions.

"Sorry, we're a bit lost too," Emily answered.

"Where exit?" the tour guide gestured with her hands looking around.

So there we were; teenagers, tour guide and two Australian tourists looking for a staircase leading down the wall and back into the city, without any luck.

"I think I see something," I called out to the group who was now following us around as though we knew what we were doing. "Over there, that dark staircase."

I walked over and peered into the darkness. Feeling brave, or perhaps reckless, I volunteered to go down and report back. Darkness enveloped me on the third step, forcing me to wait until my eyes adjusted before taking another step down.

My heart was beating slightly faster than normal, but I pretended I wasn't scared of the dark.

"Are you ok down there?" Emily's voice echoed down the stone walls of the staircase.

"Yes," I called back loudly. "I can see a small light further down. I think it leads to an open area outside. I'm going to have a look."

"Be careful!" Emily urged.

I kept my hands firmly on the stone walls as I carefully made my way down.

Yes! I was exuberant. *It's an opening onto a street!* I paused on the last step and turned my head to shout up the stairs that I had found a way, but a movement in the shadows caught my eye.

My head snapped towards a shadow detaching itself from the darkness.

"Eeeeehhk!"

A high pitched squeak bounced off the walls and it took a second for me to realise I had made that sound.

"Noor? Noor??" Emily called anxiously. "Are you ok?"

The shadow stepped into the light coming from the opening. An un-kept older man stared at me with a scowl. "Where you think you going?"

I stammered something that may have sounded like "lost – directions …don't know -what is this place ...?"

Amazingly, he seemed to understand me. "This no exit. Stair more ahead."

"Noor?? Why aren't you answering? I'm coming to find you!" Emily announced.

"Thank you, sorry …didn't mean to - bye …" I babbled awkwardly and made a hasty retreat up the stairs to find Emily carefully making her way down.

"What happened? Why did you scream?"

"A man appeared out of nowhere," I mumbled, a little shaken by his sudden appearance.

"What?! What man?"

"I don't know, maybe he lives there."

I stepped into the bright sunlight and was immediately surrounded by the American teenagers and their tour guide.

"Are you alright?"

"Are you hurt?"

"Why did you scream?"

Back in the open air and bathed in sunshine, the man's appearance in the dark staircase didn't seem so frightening and I, blushing and feeling very silly, told the anxious group what happened. Passing on the old man's directions, we left the tour group behind and walked until we reached the end of the rooftop walkway near the Western Wall. In the background, the golden dome of Al-Aqsa mosque was shining brilliantly in the midday sun, as the beat of joyful tambourins echoed on the breeze.

"Look down there, there's people dancing in the street. Do you think it's a festival?" I asked.

"Maybe. Let's have a look."

A bored looking young man was sitting on a low stone wall, fiddling with a video camera.

"Shalom," I waved. "What's happening over there? Is it a festival?"

"No, not a festival" he answered with a smile. "It is huge Bar-Mitzvah. It is tradition; many families have Bar-Mitzvah here at the same time. That is why there are so many people. It is a holy site so many people want to celebrate important event here."

"Ah, I see. Thank you so much," I smiled and turned to watch the celebration.

I could see what he meant, it was full of families dancing and singing, with thirteen year old boys being lifted and carried around on their father's shoulders while others danced around them. I felt privileged witnessing such a joyous occasion. Jerusalem was alive and I was elated to be part of the life surrounding me.

. . .

WE WALKED BACK to our hotel through the Jewish quarter of the Old City.

"Hi Ahmed," I said cheerfully.

"Hello, hello! How did you sleep?"

"Fine, thank you. Is our room ready for us to check in?"

"So sorry, not yet. Australian family with children staying there. They will leave soon and we will clean it for you."

"Oh, ok. Can we keep our luggage here in the lobby?"

"Yes. No worry, I look after it," he smiled through his big bushy beard.

"Thank you so much," Emily told him. "We'll go have lunch and come back later."

"We need some hours to clean," Ahmed said apologetically. "Come back afternoon."

"Ok, no problem," Emily said with a smile.

We stepped out of the hotel and into the chaos that reigned in this lane. I was beginning to think it was the busiest street in the Old City. Nowhere else we had seen was this busy. Or loud. I loved it!

"What would you like to have for lunch?" Emily asked, looking around.

Mounds of brightly coloured spices, mouth-watering sweets, raw meat and fish hanging from hooks with flies landing on them...

"How about falafels?"

"Sure, I like falafels. Should we try to find a falafel shop around here? Or go back to the New City? There were lots of falafel shops there."

I shrugged. "I don't mind. If we go back to the New City, we can do some shopping."

Emily grinned and clapped her hands. "Yes! Let's go back to the New City. I saw lots of pretty souvenirs in the shop windows there."

This time we didn't need to consult the map and made our way up Jaffa street without getting lost. With so many falafel shops around, we chose the closest one which served Israeli style falafels. Crisp pickled vegetables, creamy tahini sauce and the fluffiest, softest, most delicious morsels of falafel balls wrapped in a small, round pita bread.

"I can't believe how good this is!" Emily said.

I was too busy stuffing my face to answer. *Yum, yum! Definitely worth the 12 shekels each!*

It was hot enough to warrant an ice-cream after the delicious lunch, and then we walked off the calories by doing some souvenir shopping of handmade artefacts by local artists. With lighter wallets, we walked back to the Old City. I wanted to visit a church and light some candles in gratitude for our safe arrival (and me not getting arrested). Although I wasn't particularly religious, it seemed like the appropriate thing to do in Jerusalem.

"What church should we go to?" Emily asked as we pushed our way through the crowd at the entrance of the Damascus Gate. We had quickly learned that waiting for our turn meant we never moved forward. If we didn't gently yet assertively push our way through the crowd, we risked being dragged along with the tide of human bodies.

"Um ..." I stumbled as someone knocked into me. "I was thinking Church of Saint Anne. According to my guidebook, it's beautiful and has the Pools of Bethesda."

"What are they?"

"Ancient waters with miraculous healing powers, or something like that."

"Sounds good. Let's stop here for a second so I can find it on the map."

I was very impressed with Emily's map-reading skills. She managed to get us there without getting lost once.

"It's beautiful!" I breathed in the scent of the flowers in the well-tended church garden. Soft singing came from inside the church, and we stepped in quietly to light some candles for our families and safe travels for us.

We took our time exploring the Pools of Bethesda (although I didn't see any actual water) and played with a kitten who had appeared in the church's garden. It looked well fed, unlike the stray cats I had spotted in the street of our hotel. They looked awfully skinny with mangy coats and kept well out of the way of humans. It was heartbreaking to see, and even worse knowing that I couldn't do much to improve their situation.

"WE STILL HAVE some time before our room will be ready. Is there anywhere you would like to go?" Emily was taking pictures of the kitten in the church courtyard while I sat on a stone bench and fanned myself with my hands.

"How about looking for Armenian ceramics? I'd love to get some hand painted artefacts as a souvenir." Emily gently stroked the kitten who was relishing the attention.

"Me too! I've seen pictures online and they look exquisite." Handmade Armenian ceramics was on my list of must have souvenirs.

"I don't want a cheap copy made in another country. I want it to be authentic," Emily said.

I nodded. "Our best chance is to look for them in the Armenian quarter. Do you think you can get us there from here?"

Emily opened the guide and looked at the map. "It shouldn't be too difficult and it's not far."

"Better say goodbye to your new friend then," I leaned down to pat the kitten.

The Armenian quarter proved harder to find than we had expected. It would have been easier to find if we had started on a journey on one of the main streets, which usually had signs with English translations. Instead, we found ourselves utterly lost in a residential area without any street name signs so we couldn't even find our location on the map.

"I think we took a wrong turn somewhere," Emily said worriedly as she studied the map and our surroundings, but I knew it was useless.

We had no way of knowing where we were. We didn't even know if we were in the Christian, Muslim or Armenian quarter. The houses all looked the same and there was no one walking around that we could ask for help.

"Let's keep walking. We're bound to find a major street at some point, or run into someone who can give us directions." I tried not to sound too worried.

So we walked, and walked but didn't see anyone or find a street sign. Three young men appeared behind us, but were too far to ask for directions so we kept walking. They seemed to be going the same direction we were because every time I turned my head, they were still there.

They probably live around here and are just going home, I told myself but couldn't help thinking, *we're outnumbered, in an unfamiliar area with no one else around.*

"An Israeli flag," Emily pointed up to a high military looking watch tower.

"Are we in the Jewish quarter now?"

"I don't know, but there is a soldier with a rifle gun up there."

"Let's stand under it and wait for them to pass. The soldier should be able to see us from up there, just in case we need help."

We stood under the tower and waited for the three young men to walk past. Perhaps they were simply on their way somewhere and it was coincidence we seemed to be going the same way. Perhaps they lived in the area. Perhaps they were very nice and kind people, but I wasn't prepared to risk our safety by giving them the benefit of the doubt.

We waited a little while before we continued walking. There was no point calling out to the soldier in the tower for directions. He was too high up to hear us. Then, somehow, we stumbled on a crowded street. We still didn't know where we were in the Old City, but at least there were people around.

"Should we ask for help?" Emily looked around at the

people walking past. Most walked right past us as though in a hurry to reach their destination.

I spotted two young Israeli guards not wearing the traditional military uniform, patrolling the area. I could tell they were some sort of Israeli military or security personnel because they wore Jewish kippas on their heads, a communication earpiece with a transmitter, sturdy military boots, a plain beige t-shirt and army looking pants, but what really gave it away was their gun. And the way the crowd reacted to their presence. People moved out of their way as they walked down the street checking that doors were firmly locked.

"We could ask them," I pointed as one pulled on a doorknob to check it was locked while the other guarded his back.

"I don't know… they seem to be busy. They might not want us to bother them."

"I'll try, and if they can't or don't want to help they can just say no."

The presence of armed soldiers or whatever they were made me feel safer. Since childhood, like most Australians, I have been taught that authority figures are the people to turn to in time of need – police officers, firemen, paramedics …It seemed much safer to trust a figure of authority rather than a complete stranger off the street.

I waited for them to stop and check another door before approaching. Holding up the map in front of me, I pointed to the Damascus Gate and asked for directions in Hebrew. The tall, dark haired one shrugged his muscular shoulders and kept walking, but his partner stayed. Shorter, blond and with kind blue eyes, he smiled and said something that was a lot more complicated than the 'straight', 'left', 'right' I had learned. Ok, no Hebrew.

"English?" I asked hopefully.

He shook his head with a smile and said something that sounded Russian.

Maybe he knows another language. I tried Italian and Spanish but no luck.

He tried Russian again but now it was my turn to shake my head and smile apologetically. We laughed together; at least we could mime and understand each other through body language.

His partner had a very surly look on his face and muttered angrily, trying to get the Russian man, who I named Alexei, to leave. Alexei shook his blond head and said something to grumpy. I definitely didn't need a translator to understand his partner's shocked, angry look and fast muttering. He was clearly not happy with Alexei. Alexei calmly replied something which didn't seem to make his partner any happier. He turned to us with a smile and took my guide book. I pointed to the Damascus Gate. We could easily find our hotel from here. He nodded and motioned with his hand for us to follow. I thought he would take us straight there, but instead we ended up following them on the rest of their patrol, stopping at every synagogue door and checking it was locked. Alexei kept turning his head back every so often to check we were still following. His partner kept shooting us angry looks until we reached the area we needed to get to. Alexei stopped and pointed out the street sign for us but I had already recognised the area.

"Thank you! Thank you so much!" I gave him a big smile and shook his hand.

He seemed pleased and smiled back. I gave a nervous nod to his surly partner and we left. I hoped Alexei wouldn't get in trouble for very kindly helping us.

"Let's not get lost in a residential area again," I told Emily. "That really scared me."

"Agreed. Next time we try to find the Armenian quarter, we'll use the main tourist roads to get there. Let's go see if our room is ready."

"I could use a rest after all this walking. My feet are throbbing," I grimaced.

· · ·

THANKFULLY OUR ROOM was finally ready, and it was bigger than expected. It really was a family room, with four bunk beds and a big double bed. It didn't take long for the beds to be converted into our wardrobes and covered with our things.

"The water pressure is a little better but the shower head is attached to a hose that keeps falling off the wall," Emily told me as she dried her hair with a towel.

I rolled my eyes, but was too tired to care much. I wanted to rest my feet as much as possible before we went out again to find food for dinner.

"Maybe we should stock up on water bottles tonight. Tomorrow is Friday, and that's a holy day for Muslims so the shops might not be open."

"We could go shopping in the Christian, Jewish or Armenian quarter," Emily pointed out.

"Yeah, but it's a lot further to carry heavy water bottles."

Emily cringed. "Good point. We'll pick up some bottles when we buy dinner."

I sat up. "Ok, my feet have semi-recovered and I'm hungry. Want to go now?"

Emily nodded and slipped on her backpack. "I saw food stalls in the courtyard just outside the Damascus Gate. Plus there is the small bakery we bought from our first night here."

"We could try some of the sweets in the shops next to our hotel. I've been eyeing them every time we walk past …"

Laughing, we stepped out into the very crowded lane. I still couldn't believe how busy it was. Both sides were lined by tiny shops with people crowding in front to buy things. They seemed to sell everything on our little lane; clothes, sweets, toys, gold jewellery, raw fish and meat, spices, phone accessories … We made our way to the Damascus Gate, past the row of five or six Israeli soldiers armed with rifles that seemed to be permanently stationed there, and walked out into the courtyard. The Damascus Gate had transformed into a busy entrance point, with none of the tranquillity I had experienced in the morning.

I loved the liveliness of the courtyard. Tourists sat on the steps to enjoy the view, locals walked past with their children and shopping, and street vendors shouted their prices to attract buyers. Some 'shops' were as basic as a blanket spread on the ground with the produce on top, while others had crates of fresh fruit and vegetables. My favourite was an old man who wheeled a cart around selling lupin beans as a snack which seemed to be popular with the locals, even children. I tried them, but didn't share the children's enthusiasm for the bitter snack.

"How about that zaatar bread with cucumber and tomatoes for dinner?" Emily eyed some plump tomatoes and crisp looking cucumbers.

I loved the idea of shopping where the locals did. "Sounds great." I grinned and wandered over to the stalls, pointing and asking prices. Everything looked fresh and delicious but the prices seemed a little steep.

"Emily, this small box of grapes is 10 shekels, but I'm pretty sure I heard someone selling them for 5 inside the city. Everything seems to cost more than the stalls inside the Old City."

"Really? Let's shop around then, I'm not in a hurry. Do you remember where you heard the cheaper ones?"

"Yes, it was a stall on the opposite side of the bakery we bought from. I saw a shop selling water bottles too, right next to the bakery."

"Oh, good. I can't believe how much we drank today. At this rate, we're going to have to buy the eight water bottle packs instead of individual bottles."

"I'm pretty sure I sweated everything I drank," I said with a laugh and led the way through the crowded entrance.

Buying fresh produce was quite an experience. I stood near the stall, waiting for my turn, which never seemed to arrive. Woman after woman, often with a bunch of children following, stepped up and bought kilos of tomatoes, cucumbers, grapes, eggplants and so on. The grocer, a tall and lean young man with close cropped hair, and his assistants, weighed and packed at an incredible speed. It seemed that the rule here was 'first come, first served' so I took a step closer to the stall and waved to let them know I wanted to buy. The grocer nodded and when he finished with his customer, signalled for me to move closer.

"Shalom," I greeted the grocer.

"Shalom. Welcome," he answered.

My backpack and pronunciation clearly gave me away as a tourist, but I really wanted to try and order in Hebrew. "Ani rotzeh shnayim *(I want two)* ...um ..." I couldn't remember how to say tomato and cucumber in Hebrew so I pointed. Smiling, he nodded and picked up a plastic bag.

"Two kilo each?"

"No, no!" I laughed. "Two only," I said pointing to Emily and myself. I ended up buying two tomatoes, cucumbers, bananas, apples and a bunch of grapes for only a few shekels. He didn't seem to mind that I wasn't buying in kilos like the locals did, and chatted to us in English. It seemed that I was keen to practice speaking in Hebrew and Arabic, but the locals seemed just as keen to practice speaking in English. Next stop was a stall that was selling all kinds of nuts for much, much cheaper than I could find in Melbourne so I bought a large bag of cashews, pistachios and almonds. A perfect snack that doesn't require fridges or washing. The only things we needed now were the zaatar bread and water.

"Ah! Hello again," the baker smiled. "You find hotel?"

I smiled back. "Yes, thank you. We loved the zaatar bread from last night. It was delicious!"

"You want more?"

"Yes, please. Two of those," I pointed to the pile of small pizzas with a zaatar herb and olive oil paste spread on top.

"No, not fresh. I give you these. Fresh now from oven."

He went to the back of his small bakery and brought out two which were still warm.

"Thank you very much," Emily told him. "It will be a wonderful dinner."

He smiled, and wrapped them up for us to take away. "You welcome."

"We'll come again," I told him and waved goodbye.

I preferred to buy from locals rather than food chains, and I liked the idea of buying from the same place. It gave me a comforting feeling of familiarity in an unfamiliar place.

Our final stop was the small shop next to the bakery to buy water. An elderly man walked out of the store to greet us and I stared at him with wide eyes. Everything about him reminded me of my grandpa, from the walking stick to the baker boy hat on his bald head. Even his smile was warm and welcoming like grandpa's.

Mum had taught me that in Lebanese culture it was polite to address older people as Jiddo (grandpa) or Tita (grandma), or Ammu (uncle/sir) and Tant (madam) if they were middle aged. I hoped it was also considered polite here.

"Hello Jiddo (*grandpa*)," I said and his smile widened. "Badna nishtri mahye (*we want to buy water*)." I pointed to the case of eight water bottles, 1.5 litres each, and he cut it in half to make it easier for us to carry.

"Shukran (*thank you*)." I lifted my set of four bottles and nodded my head goodbye, but as I was about to walk out of the shop, he tugged at my backpack and closed the zip all the way. He couldn't speak English so he gestured to help me understand his Arabic. I grinned and thanked him, feeling a little teary and suddenly missing grandpa.

"What was that about?" Emily asked curiously.

"Pickpockets," I told her.

"What?"

I laughed. "He told me off for not closing my backpack properly and warned me of pickpockets who target tourists."

Emily laughed. "He's so sweet! People here are so friendly and welcoming."

I nodded and shifted my four bottles so I could carry them easier through the crowded lane towards our hotel. My plan was to email my family (if the internet was working), have a picnic dinner and go to sleep early. It had been a long day of many kilometres of walking, and I was still recovering from jet lag.

As TIRED AS I WAS, I didn't fall asleep right away. I could faintly hear the noise from the street just below the window and I smiled. I liked being part of the chaos and life that was the Old City of Jerusalem. I had enjoyed my time in the New City in the morning, but found it to be quite European. I hadn't expected to see boutiques, gelato stores, open piazzas and musicians playing inviting tunes on cellos. The Old City, with its open air markets and mounds of spices and sweets, was much more exotic and closer to my expectations of Jerusalem. I was fascinated by these two cities, which co-existed independently and yet were a part of each other. I couldn't wait to keep exploring them tomorrow.

CHAPTER 5

A TALE OF TWO CITIES

THUMP THUMP THUMP.

My eyes flew open.

It was still dark.

Must have been a dream, I told myself and rolled over to go back to sleep.

"Did someone knock?" Emily mumbled sleepily.

Now I was wide awake. "You heard it too?" I sat up and grabbed the alarm clock next to me, squinting to make out the numbers without my glasses. "It's 3.30 am! Who the heck is knocking on our door??"

"Maybe it's a fire drill or something?" she suggested.

I got up and made my way to the door in the dark, and pressed my ear against it. "I can hear someone knocking on the other doors…"

Loud chanting penetrated the thick hotel walls.

"What on earth is that?!" I asked Emily.

"Oh! It must be the call to prayer!"

"The what? It's 3.30 in the morning!"

"I think the hotel staff knock to wake up guests, to remind them of prayer times."

"I don't think they need to knock to wake guests. The singing from the mosque's loudspeaker is like they are right here." I walked over to the window and lifted the curtain. It was dark outside, and although I couldn't see any mosque nearby, I could hear the direction it was coming from. They must have incredibly powerful speakers.

"I'm going back to sleep," Emily yawned.

I sat on the bed to wait for silence. For the first fifteen minutes I was charmed to experience this local custom, but it didn't stop for another fifteen minutes. By then, I was downright grumpy and just wanted to get back to sleep. I couldn't believe how loud it was!

By THE TIME we woke up and went downstairs to the lobby, the other hotel guests were up and about. I had noticed last night that most of the guests seemed to be very religious Muslims. The men wore the white gowns and caps while many of the women were completely covered and only showed their eyes. There were only a few other Europeans besides us.

No wonder they were so suspicious at the airport. Maybe I should have booked in the Armenian or Christian quarter and saved myself hours of stress. I was grateful I had made it past airport security.

"Ready for another day of exploring?" Emily asked brightly.

"You bet!"

We stepped outside and the usually chaotic lane was practically deserted. None of the shops were open so we decided to go to the New City for breakfast. The Jewish Sabbath (Shabbat in Hebrew) didn't start until sunset so I was hoping the shops would be open during the day. When we got there the stores were just beginning to open but people were already rushing about getting ready for Shabbat.

"What is that delicious aroma?" Emily sniffed the air.

I licked my lips. "Whatever it is, I want it."

It was an incredibly tantalising aroma. We followed our

noses to a quaint little French bakery with a delicious array of cakes, tarts, biscuits and sweets. The baker, a tall, lean elderly man, was speaking French to one of his customers while we agonized over what to choose. I was tempted to buy one of everything. As tonight would be our first Shabbat in Israel, it seemed fitting to buy Challah bread, (bread traditionally eaten on the Sabbath).

We sat at one of the tables outside, enjoying the sunshine and superb Challah bread.

"Where do you want to go next?" Emily asked, offering me the loaf.

I broke off a large piece and closed the guidebook. "How about we let fortune guide us? We could just walk and see where we end up. There's plenty of street signs here so we'll be able to find our way if we get lost."

Emily nodded and we walked around rather aimlessly, happily munching on Challah bread. By chance we ended up in front of an Italian synagogue which was surrounded by restaurants with Italian names like 'Pera e Mela' ('Pear and Apple'), selling pizza and pasta. The street looked like it belonged on a postcard from Italy. The architectural style of the houses, the flowers hanging in pots from balconies and the décor looked Italian. To complete the atmosphere, musicians playing classical music sat in an open courtyard, which could easily be mistaken for a piazza in Rome. Everything was so picturesque! Jewellery and clothes stores sold luxury items, cafes` with outdoor tables and seats lined the streets, antique looking lampposts decorated the sidewalks, and people strolled around, looking fashionable and carefree, with their well-groomed dogs. Everything was very prettily displayed inside shop windows. No one shouted out the prices of their wares and there was plenty of space to walk without getting bumped by the crowds. It was all very neat and orderly. I liked it but it reminded me too much of home, especially when I saw the large McDonalds store. I found myself missing the chaos and noise of the Old City.

· · ·

BACK IN THE OLD CITY, we headed to The Armenian quarter and this time, we didn't get lost! We entered through the Jaffa gate and found ourselves in a large open square. To my left was a Christian information centre, a money exchange store and just ahead was a narrow market lane. It was spotlessly clean, spacious and bright. Very different to the crowded and narrow lanes I was quickly becoming used to in the Muslim quarter.

Emily tapped my arm and nodded her head towards a couple of trolleys loaded with mouth-watering sweet bread stuffed with dates and the savoury, sesame covered, bread I adored. I grinned and nodded. I loved buying from the street stalls like the locals did. It was delicious and I preferred to give my money to small businesses rather than big supermarket chains, or cafes and restaurants designed for tourists.

"This date bread is delicious!" Emily offered me a piece to try.

"This would be great with a cup of tea. Try some of the savoury one; it's so fresh and fluffy."

"We should get more and for tomorrow's breakfast," Emily suggested. "In case we can't find open shops to buy from."

"And some more fruit and nuts. I saw a market stall near the hotel lane that had small hills of all kind of nuts."

Emily pulled out the guide book and opened the chapter on the Armenian quarter. "We can walk down this lane, turn right and then be in the Jewish quarter."

An older man made his way over to us with a smile.

"Where you want to go? I will take you."

How kind! He thinks we are lost and wants to help.

"No thank you, we know where we are going," Emily answered.

"You look lost."

"We just got here and want to look around. We have a map," I told him with a smile.

"Have you seen Mount of Olives? I take you there. You know, Jesus was there. Where you want to go, I show you all Jerusalem! I am tour guide."

The smile fell off my face. *Hmpf. I thought he was being kind but he wants business.* "Thank you we have a tour booked, we're just walking around today," I told him in what I hoped was a polite yet firm tone before walking away.

Does approaching strangers like that actually work? Do people randomly get in a car with a complete stranger who promises to take them somewhere? It just seemed so dangerous to me.

"Want to walk through the market lane and look at some shops?" Emily asked.

I nodded and followed her. Small stores with brightly coloured pottery lined each side of the laneway, all with an eager salesman at the entrance.

"Good morning! Welcome, welcome!'

"Good morning, welcome please! Come look, beautiful things I have."

I made the mistake of responding good morning to a few, which they took to mean I was interested in their merchandise.

"Come see my store, I see you looking – I have beautiful things, anything you want! Looking is free! Come see, come inside!"

A polite nod of my head and averted gaze had been enough to discourage the others from continued efforts to sell to us, but this man was very determined.

"You know, I tell you something. It tradition here that first sale of day bring luck for all day and you my first customers! You bring me luck all day if you buy from me!"

"Thank you, but we are not shopping today," I told him firmly.

The plan was to look around the stores, then come back and buy things another time. It would be impractical to buy now anyway. We would either have to carry fragile and heavy items around, or go back to the hotel to put them in our room. Besides, we still had a full day in Jerusalem so there was no rush to buy.

"Yes, yes," he insisted standing right in front of us and blocking our way. "Look around my store. Come see, you look and then decide if you buy or not. My business not going well lately, buy and bring me luck."

Now I felt guilty. What if he was telling the truth and his business really was doing badly?

I can always come back and buy from him later. Besides, it's so deserted here it looks like the other shops aren't doing much better. Even if I spent all my money here, it wouldn't be enough to help them all. I comforted myself that it was still early in the morning and it might get busier during the day.

"I can see that you have beautiful things, but we really don't want to buy today. Thank you." I tried to step past him but he blocked me.

"Ok ok, come look, just one minute – you will bring me luck if I sell."

A little annoyed, but also curious about the merchandise available, I realised the quickest way to get rid of him was to humour him and step inside for a moment. Big mistake. I should have just kept walking, but now that we were inside, he was determined to sell something. The store was over-crowded, with merchandise stacked on top of each other. He did have a large range available; everything from Armenian ceramic candle holders, to dinner sets and Israeli coloured glass. I made a mental note of some lovely items I would like to buy as souvenirs for my family, thanked him, and started heading out of the store.

"Oooo not going to buy anything? My first sale for the day! I am very disappointed in you, you are very hard women – very hard women to sell to, very disappointed."

"I told you we are not buying today." I was really getting annoyed now. I hate being pressured into things. All the other shop keepers were watching and some were laughing.

"Take my card, when you want to buy come back to me," he ordered.

I took it reluctantly but knew I would not come back. I didn't like his sales technique of emotional manipulation, or his pushiness. "Thank you, goodbye."

He watched us leave from the entrance of his store, shaking his head with an annoyed expression and complaining loudly that we were hard women to sell to. The other shopkeepers were laughing at his failure. I walked through the rest of the market lane trying to avoid making eye contact with the storekeepers, or looking too long at an item on display, even if it caught my attention. I couldn't help noticing how empty this market lane was; few tourists seemed to venture this way because it was not as close to some of the holy sites in the Old City as other open air markets. It made me wonder whether the old salesman was telling the truth after all, and I felt slightly guilty for not buying from him. *It might get busier,* I reminded myself. In any case, it would not be fair to buy just from him and not the others.

I wasn't sure what to think of The Armenian quarter. The most noticeable difference was the complete lack of Israeli soldiers or armed guards. It looked poorer than the Jewish quarter, cleaner than the Muslim quarter, and less crowded than the Christian quarter. It looked a little abandoned and for some reason I couldn't work out, it made me feel sad.

TURNING the corner at the end of the lane, we found a series of smaller stores that looked like someone had carved holes in the city walls and added shelves. These stores were so small you could not comfortably fit more than three people inside at the same time. They were all selling the same thing; Armenian ceramics. Unlike their colleagues in the market lane, these shopkeepers smiled and said hello but didn't try to pressure us to buy. The last little shop was open, but there was no shopkeeper in sight.

"Where's the shopkeeper? I want to look at those candle sticks."

"He might have gone to the bathroom, and will be back in a minute," Emily said.

I looked at the neighbouring shopkeeper who was sitting in a white plastic chair outside his shop. "Open?" I indicated to the abandoned shop, thinking it might be part of his.

"Welcome, welcome," he said and indicated for us to go in but didn't get up from his chair. He called out loudly "Majd!" When no answer came, he stood up and spoke to the other shopkeepers who started calling out "Majd! Majd!"

I looked at Emily and she shrugged her shoulders. I could hear footsteps pounding on the stone ground and a young boy with reddish hair and flushed cheeks ran straight towards us.

"Welcome, welcome. Please come in, look and see what you like."

I tried to hide my surprise. Was he the shopkeeper? Why was such a young boy running his own stall, when he should be at school or playing with his friends? He couldn't have been more than eleven years old at the most. He seemed a little shy and quiet, with fair skin, intelligent light brown eyes and a soft spoken voice. He didn't look much like the rest of the local population I had seen. We walked in and he rushed around the store with a rag to clean a thick layer of dust from the merchandise.

There was something heartbreaking about the store and the young salesman. Everything was covered in a thick layer of dust, a testament to the almost hidden location of his store where few tourists explored. It was very obvious he had not made a sale in a while. I picked up the candles sticks I had seen and admired their colour.

"Please, this one is not real Armenian. It is made in

China." Majd hovered nearby. "This is handmade and painted Armenian ceramic. Much better quality."

I raised my eyebrows in surprise at his honesty, put down what I was holding and picked up the candle holders he had pointed out. He was so young and gentle, a stark contrast to the pushy older men who dominated the stores nearest to the tourist sites. He seemed more honest too.

"Where are you from?" he asked shyly.

I smiled. "Australia."

"Ah, Australia! Very far away. Welcome!"

"Thank you. Your English is very good!" I couldn't believe how well he spoke, and with hardly any accent.

"Thank you." He blushed and looked down in embarrassment, busying himself by dusting items with his sleeves.

I could feel myself growing more concerned about him. Where were his parents? Did he have any? Was he the main income earner for his family? Maybe he was just helping out for the day? I wanted to ask him, but it seemed rude and personal.

"You have beautiful things," I complimented.

There was much less variety than the other stores we had seen, but I didn't care. I had already decided I was going to come back another time and buy from him. It was clear that his business needed my holiday money a lot more than that pushy salesman, who was organised enough to have a beautiful business card.

"We are in Jerusalem for another day so I will come back and buy from you another time," I promised him.

"Yes, thank you. Welcome."' He smiled sweetly and quietly went to sit in the white plastic chair at the front of his store.

My heart ached at this sad sight. *I will buy all my ceramic souvenirs from him*, I promised myself. Emily had finished looking at the merchandise and we walked a few meters down the lane before she stopped and opened the guide book.

She looked at the map and around the lane we were in with a furrowed brow. "We should be on the border of the Jewish quarter."

"I can't see any sign that says 'Entrance to the Jewish quarter', unless there isn't one?"

"Excuse me, can I help you?" Majd called out.

He got off his chair and walked over to us.

Emily smiled at him. "We are trying to find the entrance to the Jewish quarter. I think we are close." She pointed to the map in the open book.

"Yes, it is right here. Just walk straight and you will see painted wall. That is entrance for Jewish quarter."

"Thank you so much," I said.

I was still struggling to understand these invisible borders between the different quarters of Jerusalem, which seemed to be more of a concept than a physical division of the city. One second you were in one quarter, and the next you were in another. The only way I could tell I was in different areas of the Old City was by the slightly different architecture, and in some cases, how clean the streets were.

"You are welcome," he smiled shyly and returned to his post in the plastic chair.

Neither of us had bought anything from him and had left with a promise of returning, which I am sure many tourists say without really meaning it, but he still came over to help us. He did not ask for anything in return. He did not pressure us to buy, and he did not use the emotional guilt tactics I detest. Such kindness, and from a complete stranger, was very touching.

"I THINK that's the entrance he was talking about," Emily pointed to a very large and intricate wall mosaic around an iron gate with two lions and, I assumed, two doves. "It's beautiful!"

I nodded while trying to take a photo that wouldn't come

out blurry. The mosaic was made up of various sections depicting different scenes, next to a smaller mosaic which had 'Welcome to the Jewish Quarter' underneath. I loved looking at mosaics, and greatly admired the patience of the artists as they painstakingly created lovely images with hundreds of small pieces of stone.

The Jewish neighbourhood was pristine and pretty. Houses and expensive looking boutiques were made of stone with a creamy hue that had a timeless look. Flower boxes adorned the windows high above, well fed cats with glossy coats miaowed a greeting as we walked past, and every now and then an Israeli flag billowed gently in the breeze. It was quiet and peaceful but I felt restless.

"I keep thinking of that little boy," Emily voiced my thoughts. She was taking pictures of the neighbourhood's cats, clearly missing her own cats back home.

"Did you notice the dust on the ceramics? It's like the shop hasn't been opened in months."

I didn't like that he was so young and working, instead of playing with friends.

"I don't think he has many customers. His shop is a little out of the way, not in a prominent tourist lane." She paused and seemed uncertain. "Should we go back and buy some things? We'll have to carry them around with us until we get back to the hotel."

"Now?" I was a little surprised because we had just started exploring the Jewish quarter.

"We don't know his store name or address to find his shop again tomorrow. We can easily retrace our steps now."

"Good point, I didn't think of that." I adjusted my backpack. I always carried two large water bottles, and while convenient, they were a bit heavy. "Let's go back. We can come back here after buying from him."

"We can walk through the Jewish quarter and it will take us back to our hotel for lunch and a break," Emily suggested.

"Yes, my feet will probably need a good rest after all this

walking. Lead on!"

MAJD WAS STILL SITTING in the plastic chair in front of his tiny store, staring at the ground and swinging his legs to amuse himself.

"Hello again," I called out.

His head snapped towards us and he jumped up with wide eyes.

"You came back!" he grinned widely. "You promise you will, and you came back!"

He beamed happiness. His smile was infectious and made me very glad I had returned. I was determined to buy enough to provide him with a bit of income, even though my suitcase was rapidly running out of room for souvenirs.

He attentively wiped off the dust on any object we touched, and searched his shelves for the matching candle-holder I was admiring. Like all the other stallholders I had come across, he was able to tell us the conversion rate for the American dollar, which was the closest to an Australian dollar, and had finished calculating the cost while I was still thinking about it (I should have paid more attention in math class). At first he was shy, standing back as I selected pieces for him to wrap up, but when he understood that I intended to buy many items, his little face lit up and he grew in confidence. He began enthusiastically selecting items he thought would interest me and kept welcoming us to his little store. He insisted on giving us a discount, which defeated the purpose of buying from him, so I selected more items hoping to make up for his loss of profit. Having bought enough to put a big smile on Majd's face, we returned to the Jewish quarter to continue exploring.

WANDERING around the Jewish quarter was a peaceful experience. It was less crowded than the Muslim quarter, with wider, paved streets bathed in bright sunlight. The buildings were a lovely sandstone colour and I loved spotting cats with glossy coats, snoozing happily on windowsills. There were more street signs with English translation, which made it quite easy to navigate most of the time. People walked around with a brisk step, preparing for the coming Sabbath at sunset, laughing and wishing each other a good Shabbat (the traditional greeting given on the Sabbath).

I couldn't help being very aware of the stark contrast between this area and the Muslim quarter where I had been staying for the last few days. One area was busy, chaotic, colourful and thrilling. The other was calm, beautiful, and exuded serenity.

We stopped to consult the map and were immediately approached by an older man.

"Hello, you lost?"

"No thanks, we have a map." I hoped I sounded both polite and firm, but he didn't seem to take the hint.

"Where you want to go? I take you. I am tour guide. I know everywhere. I take you to Mount of Olives where Jesus was. Very close, I take you in my car."

My mouth was opening and closing like a fish, trying to get a word in but he was a champion talker. I seized my chance when he stopped to take a breath.

"No, thank you. We have plans."

"Ok, ok. You tell me where you want to go and I drive. Give good price."

His persistence both amused and irritated me.

"We like to walk," Emily told him politely and started to move away and I quickly followed.

We stopped on the other side of the street to look at our map in peace, thankfully ignored by the locals going about their daily business. They must be so used to the thousands of tourists walking among them every day that the tourists seemed to blend into the background, unnoticed and invisible.

"I think we need to go this way to get back to our hotel," Emily read the map.

"Excuse me, do you need help?" A soft voice with an elegant English accent spoke.

I looked up at a young woman with bouncing brown curls, grey eyes and a warm smile. She wore a backpack too. Tourist or local?

"We need to get back to the Damascus gate," Emily told her.

The young woman nodded, her curls bouncing cheerfully and gave us clear directions on how to exit from the Zion Gate. I waited for a request for money but it didn't come. We chatted for a bit about Britain and Australia, our trips so far and wished each other a good journey.

Lunch was glorious. A simple zaatar bread (shaped like a pizza), with fresh tomatoes and cucumbers from the same stalls we bought from yesterday, eaten on the rooftop of our hotel. The steep staircase that seemed to go on forever was well worth the climb for the 360 degree view of the Old City. The rooftop, flat like most buildings seemed to be in the Old City, had been converted into a shady terrace with tables, an ornamental well and small bridge over a fake river bed. As hot as it was, I was comfortable in the shade and enjoyed the breeze that carried the noise from the street below. I could have stayed there all afternoon, but we had already made plans to explore the Christian quarter before joining the weekly Procession of the Cross. According to my trusted guide book, Franciscan monks lead pilgrims every Friday to pray at all the Stations of the Cross, where Jesus stopped along the way to his crucifixion while carrying the cross. A must see event in the life of Old Jerusalem, according to the guide book.

I didn't make it far into the Christian quarter before I was convinced by an old man sitting on the ground, to buy one of the necklaces draped over his arm. He told me business was bad and he needed the money, and that he had made everything himself. Maybe he used that line on all the tourists, or maybe he was telling the truth. In any case, my mum was about to receive a multi strand coral necklace (although, I doubted it was real coral), and a matching red bead bracelet with a Hamsa talisman attached, to protect her from the evil eye. To thank us for purchasing from him, the old man gave us directions to find the first station of the cross so we could join the procession. Just as well, because we had been wandering around for several minutes trying to find it. I would have thought that something as religiously important as a Station of the Cross would be easy to find, but many were obscure and almost hidden from sight.

He wasn't the only one to make a profit from me that afternoon. We were following the old man's directions and walking down a lane full of shops and few tourists, when a young man ran out of his store, straight towards us and blocked our path.

"Excuse me! Excuse me, can you help me please?" He shouted in English, waving the blank piece of paper in his hand.

"What's wrong?" I asked anxiously.

"How do you spell phenomenal?"

"What?!" I turned to look at Emily who seemed to be as baffled as I was.

"I really need to write this word but don't know how to spell it. Please help me, write it down for me."

"Um ...ok, well, I'm not sure how to spell it ..." I couldn't believe this is what he was so worked up about.

"It's ok, I know how to spell it," Emily told him. "I'll write it down for you."

"Thank you so much! I just have to borrow a pen. I'll go to my cousin's shop, he is next to me. Please, wait in my shop. I will be right back." He ushered us into his shop and disappeared.

I looked at Emily and we started laughing.

"Well, that's not what I was expecting when he ran up to us," she said.

"I thought it was an actual emergency, not a spelling question."

"He's taking a long time to borrow a pen," Emily observed.

"Yeah …" I was slightly suspicious, but mostly distracted by the beautifully crafted jewellery on display. "Is this the roman glass jewellery you were telling me about?"

"Yes! Isn't it beautiful?"

I nodded and leaned in to admire a pair of earrings that had bewitched me.

"I found pen!" The young man announced from the door-way. "I am Dashdash." He placed the paper on the counter and handed the pen to Emily.

"This is Emily and I am Noor."

"Nice to meet you! Welcome! Welcome to Jerusalem and welcome to my little shop."

Emily wrote down 'phenomenal'. "All done, hope it helps." We turned to leave but Dashdash dashed in front of us.

"Thank you so much for your help! To thank you, I will make you a pair of blue stone earrings to match your bead necklace."

"Oh it was nothing, you don't have to do that," Emily protested.

"No, no I insist! You helped me and now I will show my gratitude like a gentleman."

He immediately started making a pair of earrings for Emily and chatted to us about general subjects. It seemed rude to stop him and leave, and we still had some time before the start of the procession so I looked around the store while Dashdash finished the earrings.

"How long have you been making jewellery?" I asked.

"I have been working in this shop with my father, since I

was eight years old. See this necklace? This is my design. And these earrings too. I design and make everything in here."

I was stunned as he looked about 19 years old and the jewellery was of a very high quality.

"I can't believe you were so young when you started. You're very good at it!"

The jewellery was beautiful, and some pieces quirky, just as I liked.

"Yes, but now I want to change business. That is why I am selling everything on sale. I want to close this shop and get the money to start my own falafel business. Or maybe go to university and do a business degree, but I haven't decided yet."

"So if I buy from you, I am funding your education or helping you setup your falafel shop?"

"Yes! Exactly!"

I laughed. The truth was, I was justifying my intent to purchase the exquisite pair of earrings that had caught my attention when I walked into the store. It was love at first sight.

The prices were high, but cheaper than the boutiques in the Jewish quarter, and the jewellery was unique. An inner debate raged in my head. I needed to economise so my spending money would last for the whole trip, but on the other hand I couldn't find jewellery like this in Australia. Vanity won over reason and logic, and we each managed to part with a hefty sum of shekels (you don't need to know exactly how much). Exuberant at his success, Dashdash now became pushy and tried to sell us more. I had spent almost all my shekels, but he was very eager to accept any other foreign currency I had. He even followed us out of the store, offering two thousand camels for my hand in marriage. Embarrassed, I laughed and waved goodbye. We were too late to join the procession at the First Station of the Cross, but Dashdash had given us directions so we could join it at the Third Station, which ended up being on the road parallel to our hotel.

· · ·

ON ONE SIDE of the street was a large group of tourists, with the devout pilgrims easily identifiable by the crucifixes they wore. On the other side, on the corner of the Via Dolorosa where we found ourselves, stood at least seven fully armed soldiers and policemen. Sunglasses, earpieces to communicate, bullet proof vests, pistols and rifles.

The sight of the weapons on display and their serious faces unnerved me. *Are they here for crowd control or to protect the crowd? Wait a minute, protection from what? Were they expecting some kind of violent attack? Perhaps on the Christian pilgrims? Maybe this wasn't such a good idea...*

"It looks like we got here before the monks. Where should we stand?" Emily asked.

"Umm... I guess here?" I was betting that the safest place was next to the armed soldiers and police, so I stood close but not too close that they would see me as a threat. They barely glanced at us, but the crowd from across the street was looking in our direction and shouting something.

"Are they talking to us?" Emily asked.

"Maybe?" I couldn't work out what they were saying.

A man stepped forward and shouted in English. "Move to the right!"

Confused, I took a step to the right.

"Move to the right!"

I took several steps to the right and looked at the crowd with a baffled expression. Why were they so obsessed with me moving to the right? I was standing in front of a wall, it's not like I was blocking their view.

"Move across street. Stand there," one of the soldiers explained.

That's when I heard chanting in Latin from around the corner and it dawned on me. To join the procession, we had to stand with the crowd on the other side of the street. Blushing, we dashed across to wait. There was a sense of eager anticipation in the air and I found myself getting caught up in the atmosphere, watching the corner of the street in almost breathless anticipation. The singing was getting louder. The dull thud of hundreds of feet on the paved street came closer. I stood on my tip toes for a clearer view and saw a monk struggling to carry a wooden cross that was larger than him. Close behind him were his brothers, chanting and leading a large group of pilgrims who were clutching their crucifixes and mumbling prayers. Some were crying. When the monks appeared, the more religious people in the crowd I stood with began to make the sign of the cross and mutter prayers. I wasn't sure what to feel – part of me was excited to be taking part in this custom, and part of me wondered how the locals felt about such a large number of Christians gathering in their street; chanting, praying and effectively shutting down the street. I looked at the locals and they were casually going about their business. Some were enjoying an afternoon break, drinking coffee and watching the procession as though it was the most mundane and normal thing in the world.

My crowd moved as one, quickly attaching themselves to the group behind the Franciscan monks and making it swell and double in size. The armed military escort moved from the other side of the street and positioned themselves around the group. We shuffled forward slowly and the monks stopped at every station to sing hymns in Latin, Italian, Spanish, French and other languages. Often, they were obscure little land-marks hidden in tiny lanes. I couldn't concentrate on the prayers so I looked around at the different shops and their bored looking salesmen. One sign had a familiar name on it, written in English next to the pretty Arabic script.

Eyes wide, I tugged at Emily's arm.

She looked at me curiously and leaned her head closer so I could whisper in her ear.

"Remember the Roman bracelet I bought? The one I ordered online from an antique dealer in Jerusalem?"

Emily nodded and looked, understandably, confused.

"I think I just saw the shop! It's that one." I tried to point discreetly, conscious that people around me were praying.

"Do you want to visit the shop later?" Emily whispered.

I nodded and made the sign of the cross with the others around me.

The monks started walking again, leading to the next prayer stop. It was stifling hot, especially in the closed laneways without a breeze of fresh air. Sweaty bodies pressed against one another. I began to wish they would hurry up.

How many more stations are there?

Overwhelmed by the heat, made worse by the numerous bodies pressing against me on all sides, I suggested an early exit to Emily. Besides, I hadn't been able to shake off the uneasy feeling of requiring an armed escort. Still, I was glad to have joined the procession, even if for a little while, and quite moved to see that the locals allowed Christian pilgrims to gather by the hundreds and perform their own religious ceremonies.

Extracting ourselves from the crowd was more difficult than I had expected, but after many "Excuse me" and "Pardon me", we managed it.

"I'm not sure where we are," Emily said, looking around the small lane.

"It's not far from the antique shop, and from there I remember how to find our hotel."

I was starting to recognise nearby streets and shops, using them as reference points to find my way to and from the hotel.

"We could stop by the antique shop on the way to the hotel," Emily suggested.

I grinned and motioned for her to follow me. When I was younger, I wanted to be an archaeologist but I ended up studying anthropology at university. I never lost my fascination of ancient civilizations so as soon as I had my first professional job; I bought an antique Roman bracelet (the only thing I could afford) from a licensed dealer. For some reason, I was very excited to see the shop where my bracelet had come from.

The noise and chaos of the outside world disappeared when I stepped into the antique shop. It was like walking into a different world, silent and mysterious. Precious artefacts were proudly displayed in glass cases, softly illuminated by small golden lights. The air was crisp and cool, a complete contrast to the humidity and heat just outside the thick glass doors.

"Welcome," a smooth, cultured voice spoke.

I looked around the empty shop.

"May I help you?" A tall man stepped out from behind a large artefact.

"Oh, sorry, I didn't see you," I babbled.

He smiled. "Are you looking for something?"

"Um, well, not really. I was just having a look …"

"You are welcome to look. We have many beautiful items."

"Yes, I know. I bought a bracelet from this shop last year."

His eyebrows raised. "Which one?"

"It was a Roman bracelet, and I had it shipped to Australia."

"Ah!" He cried out, his smile widening into a grin. "Australia! I remember you!"

"Really?"

"Yes, of course. We don't get many orders to Australia. Please, come look. I will show you some rare pieces."

"Oh, thanks but I don't think I can afford to buy anything in here."

He laughed. "Do not worry, just enjoy looking."

"Alright, thanks."

Emily amused herself looking at various pieces she would buy if she won the lottery, while Fahad showed me around the shop, patiently explaining the origin of the pieces and stories attached to them. I was fascinated and he seemed pleased by my enthusiasm. When we left, Fahad stood waving goodbye at the front of his shop until we were out of view.

OUR HOTEL LANE was crowded and busy, as it usually was, but this time my eyes were drawn to a small open door instead of the stalls of brightly coloured sweets. A middle aged man sat on a plastic chair outside, looking very solemnly at the small group of American tourists. I moved closer and to my great surprise, learned that it was one of the Stations of the Cross. A small, modest Church that I had walked past numerous times in the lane of our hotel, without realising what it actually was. The holy, hidden in plain sight among mortals.

"Emily, I think it's one of the Stations of the Cross."

"I never noticed it there! The door was always closed."

"Want to have a look?"

"Yes, let's have a look while there aren't many people to crowd it," Emily said.

Without thinking, I followed the group of Americans into the Church. It was a tiny room with stone walls. A large crucifix on the altar dominated the room, and there was hardly any room to move around the wooden pews filling the space.

"Please!"

I turned around to find the man from outside, who I presumed was the custodian of the Church, waving his hands, clearly agitated.

"Please, this holy place! Cover arms!" he indignantly pointed to my bare arms.

It was so hot, and I had gotten so comfortable in Jerusalem, that I wandered around in my long skirts and sleeveless tops. I just couldn't bring myself to wear my cardigan unless I had to and until this moment, no one had objected. Well, except for some ultra-orthodox Jewish men who covered their eyes with their hand and ran past me, or crossed to the other side of the narrow lane. I had seen them do the same with women who were wearing long sleeves and pants instead of skirts. Clearly, there were certain expectations for female clothing in Jerusalem that I was still becoming familiar with.

"So sorry," I mumbled and we dashed outside to put on our cardigans before walking back in.

"Thank you," the man said approvingly. He wasn't having as much luck with the young American woman who was also dressed in a sleeveless top. She was still refusing to cover her shoulders and after asking, in a rather demanding voice, several more times, the man went outside with a face like thunder.

Unfortunately, neither of them seemed willing to see the situation from each other's point of view or compromise. The man was adamant that baring our arms in a holy place was disrespectful, but Westerners have different standards and understanding of modesty and respectful behaviour. Shame, but I was not in Israel to pursue world peace so I left them to sort it out between themselves and continued to the hotel for a rest.

THERE WAS TOO much to see in the Old City so we didn't rest for long. As soon as my feet had stopped throbbing enough for me to walk, we went in search of The Dome of the Rock. We had seen the golden dome shining in the sunlight from our hotel rooftop and were keen to get a closer look. One of the reasons we had chosen the hotel we were staying in was because of its proximity to major tourist sites, including the beautiful Dome of The Rock. We easily found one of the entrances listed in the guide book, partially hidden at the end of an open air souk lane. A big, muscled guard stepped in front of us.

"Where you go?"

"Um, we are going to see The Dome of The Rock." I nervously showed him the pictures in our guidebook.

He shook his head. "Closed now. Only Muslim can go through here. You go through here," he pointed to the Western Wall Plaza on the map.

"Oh, ok. Thank you." Disappointing, but we could try again tomorrow.

He went back to sentry duty at the lane entrance, and we went in search of an early dinner.

THE OLD CITY never failed to provide entertainment and memorable experiences. Strolling through the markets was a thrilling experience. Locals would barter loudly to get bargains, young Israeli soldiers would stand around joking with each other (and occasionally get told off by their commanding officer), and the young local men would try to flirt with women walking past, regardless of whether they were locals or tourists.

It was a lovely evening. The refreshing breeze was particularly welcome after a blistering hot day. Waiting for our pizza to be ready, we sat at the front of the strategically placed café facing the corner of the Via Dolorosa. On one side was a small troop of Israeli soldiers (that street corner always had at least three soldiers stationed during the day) and right next to them was a Christian hospice that seemed to be the gathering spot for local teenage boys trying to flirt with girls. They were particularly high spirited this evening, laughing loudly and pushing each other playfully. Time after time, a tourist would open the hospice door and almost trip on the teens sitting on the front steps. I couldn't help chuckling a little. It seemed that wherever you went in the world, teenagers were the same.

Close by, a few young men stood leaning against the wall of a building, their eyes following a veiled Muslim woman as she walked past with her three, young unveiled teenage daughters.

One of them called out a greeting. "Marhaba."

"Marhaba," the mother responded politely as she walked past.

Emboldened, the young man flicked his cigarette ashes and took a step forward.

"Tfaddalu," he called out eagerly, inviting them to make themselves comfortable.

Blushing, the young teenage girls shot him a quick side glance while their mother turned her head to look at him and pertly replied, "Wein, al sahra? *(Where? On the rock?)*." This sent her daughters into a fit of giggles and I, having shamelessly eavesdropped on the whole conversation, burst out in loud laughter. Emily, and the people sitting near us, stared at me in surprise.

"What's so funny?" Emily asked curiously.

I couldn't stop laughing, but somehow managed to translate enough for Emily to understand and laugh along. The young man's look of surprise at the mother's response was priceless.

Serves him right for being cheeky, I thought to myself, still laughing heartily.

"Pizza is ready," the café owner spoke over my shoulder.

"Thank you, it smells great!" I turned to take the box off him and the smile fell off my face. The man was holding the smallest pizza I had ever seen.

"Enjoy!"

We had already paid so he didn't waste any more time on pleasantries and returned to greeting new customers as though they were dearly loved friends, while an old man prepared the food in the kitchen.

Emily opened the pizza box lid. "Well, at least they got the order right and it's vegan."

My rumbling stomach was not amused. "35 shekels! We paid 35 shekels for a pizza that wouldn't satisfy a toddler!"

"It's way overpriced for the area we are in. Did you notice that most of the customers here are tourists?"

"Hmpf. We should just follow the locals and eat where they do. I might have to buy a falafel after this …"

I stared sadly at the shrivelled up, sparsely scattered vegetables. Thank goodness the local falafel stand was close by, delicious and cheap. I could get a falafel with chips and a can of coke for 6 shekels. It might be a street stall, but the falafels were simply superb. Crisp on the outside and fluffy on the inside, cooked fresh in front of me. No way I was coming back to this tourist trap of a café`.

"Let's pick up some more water bottles, and some veggies and fruit to snack on," I suggested to Emily. Another hot day of drinking litres of water, only to sweat it out almost immediately. Besides, I liked buying from the old man who looked like my grandpa, and the grocer from across the street who by now recognised us and waved hello when we walked past. I didn't know their names, but their friendly wave made me feel welcome in this ancient city full of strangers.

IT WAS A LOVELY EVENING, and the best way to enjoy the cool evening breeze and sunset was on the hotel rooftop. From there I could see the whole city. I loved climbing up during the day to watch Jerusalem live, and at night, with the stars above me and the cool breeze blowing, watching the city gently drift into a peaceful sleepiness. Tonight was different. The atmosphere was boisterous and the streets still crowded. It was Friday night, and the Muslim quarter had come alive with laughter and happy chatter.

Emily and I leaned over the rail, peering into the street below.

"It sounds like a party down there. Let's go down and have a look," Emily suggested.

"Ok," I cheerfully agreed. It was still light, and I knew the Israeli soldiers would still be stationed at the entrance of the Damascus gate and on the corner of the Via Dolorosa, so I felt safe exploring for a little while.

All the small shops in our street were open and the locals lingered in the narrow street, chatting and enjoying the beautiful weather and slower evening pace. We walked to the end of the street which led to the Damascus Gate entrance. The young soldiers on duty looked relaxed and calm, but kept an eye on the crowd. It seemed like hundreds of people were walking through the entrance of the Damascus Gate.

Hot, sweating bodies were pressing against me on all sides. Vendors shouted their prices and locals shouted greetings to each other. I cringed and rubbed my ears, my eyes scanning the crowd for Emily's familiar dark hair and bright clothes. Planting my feet firmly on the ground, and hoping I would not be swept away by the tide of bodies, I waved frantically to get her attention and pointed to the gate. Emily nodded and began to walk against the tide of people coming through. I followed, slowly, constantly apologizing to the people I inevitably bumped into. Several more apologies, being pushed back by the crowd and pushing my way forward, I made it out into the courtyard in front of the Damascus Gate and sighed in relief. There was a steady stream of people walking from the direction of the New City and heading for the gate, but in the large, open space of the courtyard, it didn't feel crowded.

"I can't believe how busy it is," Emily said with wide eyes.

My face was red from the exertion and my throat was bone dry.

"Water break?"

I joined the other tourists and some locals, sitting on the steps and enjoying the comings and goings of the Old City.

I pulled out the water bottle from my backpack and gulped it, then splashed some on my face to try and cool down. As heavy as the two litre bottles were to carry around in my backpack, I never left the hotel without them. Even though I lived in Australia and my mother is from the Middle East, I struggled to cope with heat.

"Are you ok?" Emily asked, her tone clearly worried.

"Yea, just got over heated when I was stuck in the crowd."

She nodded understandingly. "I'm happy to just sit here and enjoy the breeze."

I smiled gratefully and stretched my legs. The courtyard was alive with activity and I loved watching it. Young boys were flying their kites while little girls sat on steps watching them, street vendors were packing up their wares and locals were stopping to chat and sit on the steps, enjoying each other's company and the evening.

I was enjoying the relaxed atmosphere when several ultra-orthodox Jews ran past us and went through the Damascus Gate.

"What's going on? Why are they running?"

So far, I had seen very few ultra-orthodox Jews walk through the Muslim quarter, especially at night after the soldiers had left their station, but here they were, hundreds of them, going through the Damascus Gate.

I turned to look in the direction they had come from and my jaw dropped. Hundreds of ultra-orthodox Jews; young, old, male and female, ran in groups straight through the Damascus Gate and disappeared into the old city. Children ran alongside their parents, and the very young ones whose little legs could not keep pace were pushed in their strollers. They all seemed to be dressed in their finest clothes; the women wearing beautiful wigs, makeup, jewellery and heels (a challenge on the cobbled streets of Old Jerusalem), while the men sported huge, round, fur hats and long black coats. One man had worn a gold coloured satin coat for the occasion, his long side locks well-groomed and swinging as he rushed past.

"Clearly, the exciting place to be tonight is in the Old City," Emily commented.

Curiosity was winning over my desire for ice-cream. "Maybe there is a festival? Should we follow them and see where they are going?"

Emily grinned and nodded.

We followed the large crowd of orthodox Jews hurrying down the Via Dolorosa, their eyes looking straight ahead, their steps quick and sure. More than the usual numbers of Israeli soldiers were stationed along the street, all looking very alert, while the locals in the Muslim quarter stood along the sides, watching this spectacle as though it was a perfectly ordinary occurrence.

We followed, with no idea of where they were heading, until we reached a familiar spot and I gasped and smacked my forehead.

"I know what they are doing," I told Emily, stepping to the side to let those behind us walk past. "This is so embarrassing, I should have realized sooner."

"What are you talking about?"

"I met a Jewish girl in Melbourne who told me about this. She lived in Israel for a while and apparently, every Friday at sundown, the orthodox Jews from Mea-Sharim walk to the Western Wall to pray. Apparently, some come here to pray every day, to prepare for the Sabbath."

"Ah, mystery solved. It's getting a bit dark now," Emily said as she watched people continue to walk past us. "We should probably go back to the hotel."

"Yeah," I agreed a little reluctantly.

I didn't know how safe it was to walk around the Old City at night, and the soldiers would be leaving their post soon. Going back to the hotel seemed like the most sensible idea.

Some adventurer you turned out to be, I laughed at myself.

We walked back at a leisurely pace, enjoying the more relaxed atmosphere along the street until we reached the café where we had bought our pitiful pizza, near the corner of the Via Dolorosa. The street was alive with the sound of tambourines, whistling, clapping, cheering and singing. I stared, a little stunned, at the hundreds of people dancing on the spot, some waving their arms in the air.

"It looks like Friday night is party time in the Old City,"

Emily said with a laugh. "Shall we move closer and have a look?"

I glanced at the Israeli soldiers stationed at the corner of the Via Dolorosa. They were leaning against the wall, talking and laughing. My shoulders relaxed and I followed Emily towards the crowd. The happy vibe was infectious and I grinned. People in the crowd were beaming, hugging each other and dancing on the spot.

"Maybe it's a local festival?" I suggested to Emily.

"Or a giant street party! Look at the size of the crowd."

"What's that?"

"Where?"

"That pole in the air...oh, it's a flag." I squinted my eyes to make out the flag in the dim light, as the pole bearer waved it about energetically.

BANG!

My heart stopped then started galloping.

BANG! BANG!

"Was that - was that gunshots?" I clenched my fists to stop my hands trembling but I couldn't hide the tremor in my voice.

The crowd began chanting while the flag waved high in the air.

Emily stood frozen, several feet away from the crowd. She looked at me with wide eyes.

BANG! BANG! BANG!

The crowd cheered and chanted louder.

I gasped. It was unmistakable. Those things being held up towards the sky were definitely guns. My heart skipped a beat then began to gallop.

I grabbed Emily's arm and practically dragged her back to the corner of the street where the Israeli soldiers were, looking calm and relaxed. My head turned from them towards the crowd and the Palestinian flag being thrust into the night sky, and back again. I couldn't work out what was happening.

"Are you ok? You look stressed."

"You heard the gunshots too, right?" I asked, surprised to see my hands trembling a little.

Emily nodded. "Yes, but the soldiers don't look worried. It must be a festival. The people in the crowd seem happy, not angry. Let's go a little closer and have a look."

My feet refused to move.

If it's a festival, why are they firing guns? Should I insist we go back to the hotel? What if the crowd's mood changes and we get stuck in a local protest?

I must have looked quite frightened because a little girl walked right up to me and spoke in Arabic. She must have been around ten years old, her ponytail bouncing as she nodded her head and patted my arms in a sweet gesture of reassurance. She kept repeating something in Arabic, but my brain was frozen and I couldn't work out what she was saying. I shook my head to show I didn't understand, so she mimicked an imaginary ring being slipped onto her finger and said in English, "Its ok."

"Oh!" I breathed in relief. "A wedding! Emily, I think she's saying it's a wedding."

The little girl grinned and patted my arm a few more times before joining her friends who were watching the festivities.

"See? I told you it was a celebration. No need to be scared."

"Yes, well, I think I have had enough adventures for today. Let's go back to our hotel," I suggested, my heart still fluttering.

"Alright," Emily agreed, but I couldn't help feeling she was a little disappointed at not seeing a local wedding.

Although the soldiers seemed relaxed and the crowd seemed happy, those gunshots had really unnerved me. The Old City was proving to be far more exciting than I had expected.

CHAPTER 6
NOTHING IS FREE

I woke up refreshed and energised, in spite of being woken up by the 3.30 am call for prayer. Today was our last day of independent exploration in Jerusalem, and we had a few things to tick off our itinerary list. After a quick breakfast of bananas and locally made nut bars, we walked up to the New City of Jerusalem for a rather urgent errand; withdrawing souvenir money from an ATM machine. It was like walking into a ghost town. The Sabbath had started at sunset last night, but I wasn't expecting the city to be so empty. Apart from a few cats lounging about, Emily and I seemed to be the only humans walking around the New City. No cars, no trams and all the shops were closed - a complete contrast to the bustling Muslim quarter just down the hill.

On our itinerary today was souvenir shopping and I knew exactly what I was going to buy; ceramics from the little boy Majd for my family, and small, wooden crosses. I wanted something authentic from Jerusalem so I was searching for the Jerusalem Cross, which looks different to the traditional, and simple design of the Catholic Cross I was used to seeing.

The afternoon had been dedicated to finding the entrance for foreigners to the Dome of The Rock. Ahmed, the concierge at our hotel, had told us that the Dome of The

Rock was open to non-Muslims on Sundays and gave us directions to the entrance. Our plan was to find it in the afternoon, so that we wouldn't waste time looking for it tomorrow morning before we left for Tel Aviv. After another delicious lunch of falafel wraps on the hotel rooftop terrace, we began walking in the direction Ahmed had told us.

"Are you sure we didn't take a wrong turn?" I asked Emily who was scrutinising the map.

"Positive. We went exactly the way Ahmed told us and the entrance should be here."

I looked around at the narrow street lined with sand-coloured stone houses. I had no idea what quarter of the Old City we were in, and the only distinguishable features were the windows high above us. Unlike other windows I had seen in the Old City, these were beautiful wooden screens that made me think of Moorish architecture.

Emily pointed to the sign on the wall. "It says 'Entrance to the Dome of the Rock', so it has to be here somewhere."

"Yeah, but the arrow underneath leads to a dead end."

"Maybe it's a small entrance and we missed it?"

I walked back to the sign and peered into the darkness of the narrow alley underneath it.

"This can't be the entrance. I think it's the local rubbish dump."

"How do you know that?" Emily asked.

"I can smell it and make out the outline of rubbish bags. Besides, it's so dark in there; it's got to be a dead end. There's no light coming through from the other side."

Emily sighed. "Let's retrace our steps to the start of the street and try again."

No mistake. We had turned into the right street, and the entrance was, according to the map and sign on the wall, very close by.

"Where you want to go?"

I looked up from the map towards the row of young men

sitting on white plastic chairs, all puffing away on cigarettes. One of them stood and walked over confidently.

"You are here," he pointed to our map. "Where you want to go?"

"We're trying to find the tourist entrance to the Dome of the Rock," I explained.

"Yes, easy. It hard to find alone because it goes between houses, but I show you shortcut. It take two minute."

His friends were staring at us, lounging in the chairs and blowing out large puffs of smoke.

"Thank you, but we don't want to be a bother," I said.

"We have a map, I'm sure we will find it soon," Emily added.

"No bother at all!' he assured us. "Really, it is no bother to me - is very close to here and will only take me two minutes! I can help you. Follow me." Without waiting for a response, he began walking towards the sign and motioned for us to follow, but we didn't move.

The young man looked at us with raised eyebrows and walked back. "Come, follow me!"

I bit my lip, thinking of how to refuse without offending him. "We really don't want to trouble you," I said again.

"No trouble, no trouble. Come."

I glanced at Emily who shrugged her shoulders. I wasn't keen on following a complete stranger, but it seemed rude to reject his help.

He walked a few steps and looked over his shoulder. I started walking, but kept enough distance from him that he kept looking over his shoulder to make sure we followed.

It was the exact same way we had walked earlier.

"I knew the entrance had to be around here somewhere," Emily commented as he walked into the dark lane with rubbish lining the sides.

"I was sure it was a dead end," I muttered.

"It was probably too dark for you to see the exit," said Emily.

A little reluctantly, I stepped into the dark and smelly alley. I couldn't really tell what it was; a narrow lane with a stone roof that could have been a house connecting the two sides? Whatever it was, I still couldn't see the exit even after walking in a little further.

"This way, come," the young man called out.

I took a few more hesitant steps, but my overactive imagination tormented me with news headlines like '*Tourist bodies found among garbage bags*' and my legs stopped moving. Emily crashed into my backpack.

I looked around the lane. It seemed to be getting slightly lighter, but I couldn't see the end of this tunnel or alley or whatever I was in. *Maybe this wasn't a good idea. We should turn back...*

The young man looked over his shoulder, and seeing we had stopped, walked towards us.

"This way," he urged, but it had no effect on me.

There was no way I was following him deeper into the alley. Not when I couldn't see a way out on the other side.

He moved closer. "Are you afraid of me?"

"Where are we going?" I demanded, trying to sound tough (and failing miserably).

"Bridge to the Dome of the Rock. Is where you want to go, right? So I am taking you there."

"How much further?"

"Very close," he assured me. "Don't be afraid, I won't hurt you." He held up his hands and took a step back. "Look," he pointed ahead and to the left. "It's just through here."

"The exit?" I said in what I hoped was a firm tone.

He nodded and took another step back, moving out of my way.

Keeping an eye on him, and my back to the wall, I took a few steps forward. Around the corner, partially hidden from view, was an open and sunny courtyard.

"Oh," I breathed in relief. "Yes, I can see it."

I blushed, embarrassed at my nervousness, but couldn't help thinking *better safe than sorry!*

I walked swiftly out into a courtyard, which was more like a large, square balcony and gasped. Shining brightly like a beacon for pilgrims, the golden dome glittered against the dusky blue sky as the sun gently sank into the horizon. The evening breeze carried echoes of the murmured prayers from the Wailing Wall, and the sound of church bells ringing. I was utterly and completely mesmerised.

"That is bridge."

"What?" For a moment I had forgotten the young man who had brought us here.

"Down there," he pointed to the large courtyard in front of the Wailing Wall where a long, wooden bridge snaked its way up into the courtyard of the Dome of the Rock. "Tourists have to use bridge."

"How do we get to the bridge from here?" Emily asked.

I listened carefully to his directions so we could make our own way tomorrow morning.

"Thank you so much for your help," Emily said.

"Yes, thank you," I echoed, feeling a little guilty about mistrusting him earlier.

Instead of being a mugger as my apprehension had cast him, he turned out to be a kind and helpful person.

"Is no trouble. Is my job as local tour guide."

"Excuse me?" I asked, thinking I had misheard.

He stood in front of us with an expectant look on his face.

A little taken aback, I looked at Emily with raised eyebrows. Shrugging, she pulled out her wallet. "How much do you want?"

"Oh, only if you want to give me a little something." He held out his hand. "Only for *your* sake, to make you feel comfortable."

To make you feel comfortable?! Why couldn't he be honest and tell us he was a tour guide?

Emily turned to me and said in a low voice, "I don't have any notes smaller than 50."

I pulled out my wallet and looked inside. Nothing smaller than 20 shekels. Oh well, it would have to do. Annoyed by his lack of honesty, I grudgingly handed over the 20 shekels for two minutes of work.

With a cheerful wave, he left us to enjoy the beautiful scenery.

WE WOKE up early the next morning and after a quick breakfast of grapes, nuts and bananas (all bought from local street vendors), we dressed in floor length skirts and long sleeved shirts.

"Don't forget your scarf," Emily told me as I sat on my overstuffed suitcase and struggled with the zip.

"Do me a favour and sit on this while I zip it closed."

Laughing, Emily pushed down on my suitcase lid while I pulled the zip around.

"Damn. Maybe I bought too many souvenirs ..." I muttered.

"I'll show you how to pack your clothes so they take up less space," Emily offered.

"Cheers!" I grabbed my scarf and followed her out of the room.

I had the route planned in my head and we took a shortcut through the lane where the antique shop was. It was deserted apart from a few shop keepers opening their stores for the day. We were almost at the end of the lane when someone shouted "Australia!"

My head snapped around. Fahed was standing at the door of his shop with a big grin, cheerfully waving.

"Where are you going so early?"

"To see the Dome of the Rock," I called back.

"Enjoy," he waved goodbye, disappearing inside his treasure trove.

I grinned, delighted with Jerusalem and its people. I was a stranger in this land, but when shopkeepers waved and called out hello, it made me feel welcome and less of an outsider.

Finding the entrance to the bridge took less time than expected and we joined the queue to pass through the Israeli security clearance, which consisted of a bag and body search and several questions. A bit early in the morning for all that, but I was sure it would be worth it.

The wooden bridge was closed on all sides like a very long rectangular box.

"I can see the courtyard," Emily pointed in front of us.

"We should probably put on our scarves before we step out of the bridge."

I draped mine over my hair in the style that some foreign correspondents wear when reporting from the Middle East. It was wide enough to cover my head and shoulders.

We stepped out of the bridge into the bright sunlight bathing a large, marble courtyard with a beautiful fountain. The golden dome of the mosque shone brilliantly in the morning light and I was already looking around for the best spot to take a photo. It was a good thing we had come early so our photos wouldn't be crowded with people. There were few tourists about and the only other people there were a couple of Israeli soldiers carrying rifles and several young men who looked like locals.

"Excuse me." One of the young men stepped in front of me.

I looked up, and up, into his round face. He looked like a bouncer at a night club; tall, heavily muscled and wearing a black t-shirt.

"I am representative of Muslim religious authority." He flashed a card in front of my nose.

"Um ...okay ..."

"I make sure visitors dressed respectfully."

I nodded, confident that my attire met the criteria. The

only skin I was showing was my face and hands, and my clothes were loose fitting.

"Take off scarf and cover your chest."

"I beg your pardon?!"

"You need to cover your chest with scarf," he repeated.

I looked down to make sure no cleavage was accidentally showing. "But …it *is* covered." My scarf was long enough that it draped halfway down my arms. I may not know much about Islam, but I did know that women covered their hair in holy places. He couldn't possibly mean that I should uncover my hair.

"Your chest," he indicated on his torso around the area where breasts would be.

I raised my eyebrows at him. *Is he really some kind of clothing police, or just trying to be cheeky?*

"You do not need to cover your hair," he explained. "Is more important to cover chest with scarf, like this." He pulled off his own scarf and wrapped it around his shoulders.

"Oh!" I blushed, realizing he meant I needed to conceal the shape of my breasts by letting the scarf drape down. Feeling rather self-conscious, I ripped the scarf off my hair and rearranged it as he had demonstrated. Emily quickly copied and we looked at him for confirmation that we were now appropriately dressed.

"Good," he nodded, but didn't move out of the way.

"This your first time visiting?" he asked with a smile. He was staring at my face, which was an improvement to him staring at my chest, but I really didn't want to prolong this embarrassing experience by chatting so I just nodded.

"Where are you from?"

I couldn't tell if this was part of the process, some form of security clearance or whether he actually had the cheek to try and chat me up!

"Australia."

"Ah, welcome."

I nodded and remained silent.

"So, are you Muslim? Because if yes, you can see inside the mosque. If not Muslim, then you cannot enter the mosque."

"No, I am not Muslim." Out of the corner of my eye, I saw the Israeli soldiers stop talking and turn their heads slightly in our direction.

"Ah, are you sure? Because you can go in if you are Muslim."

I stared at him, a little baffled. "I'm sure. I am a Christian." He was smiling and seemed in the mood to keep chatting, but I was starting to lose my patience. We didn't have much time before we had to return to the hotel for our taxi ride to Tel Aviv, and I wanted to take photos.

"Can we go now?" I said quickly when he opened his mouth to say something.

"Yes, yes sure." He stepped out of the way slowly. "My name is...' he began, but I had already walked past him and didn't want to encourage him by looking back.

"What's with the frown?" Emily asked.

"Oh, it's nothing," I said quickly and plastered a smile on my face.

I didn't want to ruin our excursion by complaining, but couldn't help feeling a little annoyed. Had he used the scarf as an excuse to stare at my breasts or was he really a local authority on tourist dress codes?

A tourist couple walked past us and my eyebrows shot up. The woman's hair was uncovered and her scarf covered her chest like us, but it was the man who had taken me by surprise. He had a scarf wrapped around him like a skirt, his pale, knobbly knees half hidden from view, and he wasn't the only male tourist walking around like that. Turns out the young man was telling the truth, which made me feel much better about my 'chest' being under such scrutiny.

. . .

I WALKED SLOWLY, stopping frequently to take pictures and savouring the sight. It was exquisite. The intricate detail of the blue tiles, the brightness of the golden top, the spacious courtyard and well-tended garden exuded peace, beauty and tranquillity. I walked around the mosque, admiring the detailed craftsmanship when black writing caught my eye. Incredibly, someone had decided to add to the décor of the mosque by scribbling a message in Arabic with a big black pen. Pity neither Emily or I could read Arabic, but I assumed by the heart shape drawn next to the message that it was some kind of love note.

Luckily Emily was keeping an eye on the time or we would have been late heading back to catch our taxi. Our organised tour started tomorrow in Tel Aviv, and we wanted to spend the day exploring the modern city before we spent the next week hopping on and off a bus.

One final check of the hotel room to make sure we hadn't forgotten to pack something, and we dragged our suitcases down to the lobby to wait for our taxi.

Ibrahim (the young man who had brought us water bottles on our first night) was talking about us in Arabic, to a concierge I hadn't met. If they had known I understood Arabic, they would not have spoken so freely.

"I'm telling you Aziz, I'm sure. I was there and I heard him make the booking," Ibrahim nodded vigorously.

"I can't believe it!" Aziz looked positively shocked and I was trying to look as though I wasn't eavesdropping.

"Yes, yes. I couldn't believe it either but that's what they agreed on. 350 shekels."

"350?! Just to take them to Tel Aviv?"

My teeth ground against each other. My gut instinct had been right. I had thought it was a steep price when Emily returned from booking it, but she had been told that was the fare for Tel Aviv. Apparently, even the locals thought it was too much.

"And the night concierge booked this?"

Ibrahim nodded. "Yes, he agreed on the price with the taxi."

Aziz shook his head in disbelief. "He will be here any minute now…"

A bald, big bellied man in sunglasses walked into the lobby. "Taxi for Tel Aviv."

"Oh, that's us!" Emily answered cheerfully while I resisted the urge to tell him to get lost.

It was too late to make alternative arrangements now, so I gritted my teeth and followed him down the stairs and out into the crowded lane. One thing was certain. He was not getting a tip!

CHAPTER 7
TEL AVIV

The charming houses built with the rosy coloured Jerusalem stone gave way to lean and modern high-rise buildings. Tel Aviv was very much a modern city with wide streets, expensive looking cars, cafes and boutique stores. Despite the traffic, the city had a very relaxed atmosphere and people walked around at a leisurely pace.

The taxi stopped in front of a luxurious looking hotel, complete with a doorman in full uniform and a beautiful beach at the end of the road. There were a few other hotels along the street, some of which looked more within our budget range. The taxi driver got out and started unloading our suitcases.

"I guess our hotel is nearby and this is the drop-off zone," I commented to Emily as we got out of the car.

"No, I think this is our hotel."

"No way! It looks like a five star hotel."

"Look for yourself," she held out our tour booking documents. "That's the name of the hotel and this is the address."

"But we booked a mid-range priced tour," I pointed out. "How could they afford to put us in a hotel like this?"

"It must be the exchange rate; one Australian dollar buys us four Israeli shekels," Emily explained.

The taxi driver had finished unloading our luggage and was waiting to be paid. I handed over the money, mumbled goodbye, grabbed my bags and walked towards the entrance.

The reception area was quite impressive. White marble floors, plush leather couches, tall vases full of flowers and all the staff were dressed in crisp looking uniforms.

"Hello, we'd like to check in please," Emily said to a slim receptionist with a short bob haircut and black eyeliner around her dark eyes. The boring black blazer and white blouse she was wearing did not dampen her glamorous aura.

"Do you have your booking?" Even her accent sounded sophisticated.

I couldn't help feeling self-conscious in this elegant setting; with my dust covered thongs (flip flops), heavy back-pack and clothes that could do with a wash. I just hadn't had time to do it in Jerusalem.

Emily handed over the paperwork and the receptionist tapped away at her computer.

"There is problem with booking," the receptionist began and my heart sank.

I knew it was too good to be true.

"They make mistake with room so we upgrade your booking."

"Thank you very much," Emily said and accepted the keys.

"If you need anything, please call reception. We have swimming pool on the roof and a gym. We hope you enjoy your stay."

I waited until we were in the elevator before I turned to Emily with wide eyes. "Did she say what I think she said? The magical word upgrade?"

"Yes she did."

"But… Why?"

"I don't know, but I'm not complaining."

I grinned. "I've never had an upgrade before."

The upgrade was adjoining rooms, each with a private

bathroom with bath tub and flat screen TVs. My room had a view of the hotel swimming pool, my own tea making kit, a desk, private phone line, mini shampoo and soaps, and best of all - a shower with strong water pressure! It made our hotel room in the Old City look like a shabby hostel.

"I can see the beach from my window," Emily called out through the open connecting door. "It's less than two blocks away."

"Where should we go first; beach or hotel swimming pool?" I asked.

"Beach," she said without hesitation. "Then the swimming pool in the afternoon. Give me a minute though, I want to freshen up first."

"Okay, I'll be in the lobby. I want to email my family and check for updates on Susi and Bruli."

IT WAS a short walk to the beach and I was soon walking bare-foot on the soft and warm sand. The refreshing breeze toyed with my loose hair as I breathed in the salty aroma of the sea. I closed my eyes to listen to the soothing waves, the laughter of children and the rhythmic sound of ping-pong balls hitting the rackets.

Wait, what? Ping-pong balls?

I opened my eyes and a hairy, naked chest walked past me, leaving me a little stunned. I looked around the beach. Bare chests everywhere, bikinis and shorts so small and tight they could be mistaken for underwear. Even the two old ladies dragging their beach chairs into the sea were wearing skimpy bikinis. The young couple playing ping pong were no exception, and for a moment I worried that the girl's bikini top could not endure the rigours of the game.

Why do I feel shocked? This is just like Melbourne.

I couldn't believe that four days in Jerusalem, where pretty much everyone dressed conservatively (in varying degrees, depending on whether they were in the Old or New City), had had such an effect on me.

"I feel very overdressed," I muttered to Emily who nodded.

We hadn't bothered wearing our swimming things and were still wearing our ankle length skirts that we wore in Jerusalem.

"What's the lifeguard shouting?"

"My Hebrew is not that good. It can't be serious though because no one is looking at him."

I headed towards the water and raised my skirt as high as decency permitted (in this case, well above my knees) and stepped into the deliciously warm water. No icy onslaught of the waves like Melbourne beaches. The water temperature here was absolutely perfect. Now I really regretted not having put on my swimwear.

"Out of water!" The lifeguard shouted in English. "No swimming!"

I froze, knee deep in the water and looked at the people swimming. They didn't look at the life guard. Neither did the old ladies sitting on chairs waist deep in the water. More people entered the water, and from their Hebrew conversation I guessed they were locals.

The lifeguard tried again, this time in Hebrew, followed by English. No one bothered to look his way. I was feeling quite sorry for him, but couldn't help laughing when he threw his megaphone onto the sand and stormed off.

Emily looked at her watch. "We should probably get some lunch."

"All right," I said reluctantly. "But let's look for a supermarket or a takeaway place close by so we can have dinner on the beach tonight."

"Yes, let's. It's so much better than eating in the hotel restaurant."

"Here," I handed Emily a map of Tel Aviv. "I picked this up from the hotel reception."

"Let's explore like we did in Jerusalem. We can look at the map if we get lost and when we want to come back to the hotel."

I slipped my thongs back on and followed Emily onto the footpath. This was my favourite way to explore a new city; unrestricted and often stumbling across hidden little gems. The only problem was I could never remember where the places were to revisit.

"Is it just me or does Tel Aviv remind you of Melbourne?" I asked, looking at the high-rise buildings and apartment blocks.

"Yes, and it seems much richer than Jerusalem. Have you noticed how many more expensive looking cars are around here?"

"All cars look the same to me," I laughed. "What do you feel like having for lunch?"

"I don't mind as long as there are vegetarian options on the menu." Emily lifted her sunglasses and looked at the menu displayed outside a falafel café. "I just want to see the price difference between here and Jerusalem."

"I don't mind having it again," I told her. "We might as well make the most of it while we're here, because they don't make falafels like this back home."

A middle-aged man with a big smile appeared at the door, as though summoned by my words. "You want falafel? Here we make best falafels!"

Emily looked at me with raised eyebrows and I grinned. It was a big claim to make and I had enjoyed some excellent falafels in Jerusalem, so this lunch would have to be very special.

"Welcome, I am Kareem. Here is menu. What you like?"

"A falafel wrap with pickled vegetables and Diet Coke for me," Emily ordered.

"I'll have the same," I said.

Kareem looked at us in surprise. "That is all? Is not much. You must eat!"

"It's what we usually have," I told him.

He shook his head. "I recommend for you. This," he pointed to something on the menu, "this and this. All very good. You must try, you will not regret."

I shot Emily an apprehensive look. The prices on the menu were much higher than the eight shekels we were used to paying in Jerusalem for a falafel lunch. At this rate it was going to cost us 24 shekels each.

"We could treat ourselves to a special lunch?" Emily suggested.

"Sure," I shrugged.

For that price, this falafel spread better be amazing.

Kareem beamed. "You will love it." He dashed off to the kitchen to place our order and soon brought out an enticing looking assortment of plates.

My hands started reaching for things as though they had a mind of their own. The falafel was crispy on the outside with a creamy soft centre, covered with tahini sauce and complimented by the tanginess of pickled vegetables, all stuffed inside soft, fresh pita bread.

Kareem sauntered to our table and looked at our empty plates with approval. "You like?"

"Oh yes," Emily told him. "It was absolutely delicious."

"I tell you, you like," he said smugly.

It wasn't busy and Kareem seemed more interested in finding out where we came from, and where we had been staying in Jerusalem than waiting on tables.

"Where you stay in Jerusalem?" He asked again, seeming both surprised and happy.

A little baffled, I repeated the name of the hotel.

"No! Is incredible!" Kareem threw his hands in the air. "They are my cousins."

"What?"

"Yes, yes. Owners of hotel are cousins of my mother." He dashed off and came back with a couple of cans of soft drink, a plate of hommous and freshly fried falafel balls. "These for you, to welcome you. All free."

"Oh, you don't have to do that," I smiled.

"I insist. You stay at my cousins' hotel and now you eat in my shop so I want to welcome you. This is Middle East hospitality."

"That is very generous," I told him with a big smile.

I didn't want to offend him by refusing his gesture of hospitality, and besides I would have been incredibly stupid to do so. The food was absolutely delicious.

"Eat, eat." Kareem urged us, watching as we scooped up the hommous with bread and bit into the falafels. "You must come back for dinner. I insist. Tonight, you will come back and eat here free as my guests."

I almost choked on the food I was chewing.

"We can't do that," Emily told him. "It's far too generous."

"No, tonight you are my guests," he insisted.

"If we eat any more today Kareem, we will explode" I told him with a laugh.

Kareem was not about to accept no for an answer, and we were only allowed to leave after promising to return as his guests for dinner, if we were hungry.

FULL TO THE point of exploding, I happily waddled around Tel Aviv. It may have been my first time here, but it felt familiar. Street lights, pedestrian crossings, trendy looking people sipping coffee at the front of restaurants and cafés.

"What on earth are all these business cards on the pavement? I can't believe someone just left them on the ground like that," I complained to Emily.

"Everything around here is so clean, I'm surprised to see litter like this," she commented.

I picked up a card and made a choking noise, halfway between a gasp and a laugh.

"What is it?"

"Umm, I'm not sure but I think it's for an escort service," I told her.

"What? That can't be right!"

"Look, it's written on here in English as well as Hebrew. 'Book sexy Israeli girls, nearby hotel rooms available'. With a half-naked woman on the card, what else could it be?"

"I can't believe it. They just dropped hundreds of cards on the pavement like that? What if a little kid picks it up?"

"Their parents are going to have a fun time explaining that," I joked.

We kept walking and found hundreds more, with different half naked women on them, scattered all over the pedestrian pavement in a few other streets. I couldn't believe it was advertised so openly, but after we walked past a marijuana smoking lounge, I decided that Tel Aviv was a very liberal city.

"My feet are getting sore," I told Emily. "Let's head back to the hotel for a swim in the pool."

"Sure, but keep an eye out for a supermarket for dinner things. I don't think I could have a meal but I wouldn't mind a nut bar and some fruit. Hang on," she stopped and picked something up from the ground.

"Another escort card?"

"No, 90 shekels," she said holding the bundle of notes in her hand.

I looked around for the owner, but there was no one nearby.

"What should we do?" She asked. "It's a lot of money."

I shrugged. "Whoever dropped it isn't here anymore. Maybe it was one of the customers from that café?"

"We can give it to the staff in case someone comes back looking for it," Emily suggested and I nodded in agreement.

We walked into the large and modern looking café with fashionable looking young people enjoying sweets and coffee. There was only one waitress on duty she was busy going from table to table, her black curly hair bouncing as she tried to balance trays of drink and food.

"Excuse me," I called out as she walked past me for the fifth time.

She looked at me over her shoulder. "Sit anywhere."

"No, wait," I called out as she walked past us again.

This time she stopped and looked at me curiously.

"We found money outside your café. Maybe one of your customers lost it?"

Emily showed her the bundle of notes. "It's 90 shekels."

She stared at us blankly. "You found this outside in front of café?"

"Yes," Emily answered.

"Why are you giving it to me?"

"In case the owner comes back for it. It was outside your café so we thought it might have been one of your customers," I explained.

Her mouth dropped open and she stared at us like we had grown a second head each. "You are giving me the 90 shekels instead of keeping it for yourself?!"

"It's not our money," Emily told her.

"You are so honest!'

Then she turned to the table next to her and spoke in Hebrew. Now the customers were staring at us with open mouths too. I shifted my weight from foot to foot and blushed. I hate being the centre of attention.

"Ok, well, um, thank you," I babbled awkwardly and turned to leave.

"No, Thank YOU! You are so honest!"

I smiled and nodded, following Emily out of the café.

"That was weird," she said when we were outside. "It's like she couldn't believe someone would hand money in."

I nodded, but was distracted by the brightly coloured shade cloths fluttering in the breeze. "Look over there, it's an open air market!"

Down the road were stalls piled high with fruits and

vegetables. Other stalls were selling clothes, jewellery and baked goods. It looked busy and I can never resist an open air market because they remind me of my childhood in Italy and Lebanon. "Want to have a look? We could find something for dinner."

"I thought your feet were sore?" Emily teased.

I grinned. "I'll soak my feet in the pool after this."

The market was much larger than the ones in the Old City, with more variety on offer. It was full of the usual shoppers one sees at a market place, mothers with children and elderly people, as well as some unusual shoppers. Walking among the crowd, chatting and giggling, were several young, female Israeli soldiers with pink handbags, which contrasted with the gun strapped to their chest. It was a much more relaxed atmosphere than the Old City, where the soldiers were all male and heavily armed.

We wandered around the market until I started limping. The piece of the thongs that sat between my toes had rubbed my skin raw and it was too late to do anything about it now. Great shoes for the beach, but not ideal for walking. Unfortunately, the pavement was too hot to walk barefoot so I wrapped some tissues around the hard piece of plastic and shuffled back to the hotel.

My poor abused feet were forgotten as soon as the elevator doors opened onto the hotel's rooftop pool. I spent a lazy afternoon floating in the pool and enjoying a view of the city and beach, only leaving when it became too crowded.

Emily poked her head in my room. "Ready to go back to the beach?"

"Almost." I gave the long skirt one last squeeze and hung it up to dry over the bathtub.

I will never take a washing machine for granted again, I thought as I rubbed my aching back.

At least now all my clothes were clean, and I could enjoy the beach without worrying about the necessity of doing laundry. I would have loved to send them off to the hotel's laundry service, but it was too expensive. Everything here seemed more expensive than in Jerusalem and I had to be careful with the money I had left.

DINNER TONIGHT WAS a small box of succulent figs from the market, with a glorious sunset as a background. The beach had been crowded during the day, but it came alive in the evening. Families with their dogs, students, couples, grandparents, cyclists and street vendors all flocked to the beach. It was like one large community party, everyone relaxed and enjoying life.

"Watch out!" Emily yelled in my ear and I ducked just in time.

Whiiiizzz the Frisbee went past where my head had been just a few seconds ago.

"Ok?" a young man holding the offending Frisbee shouted.

I gave him a thumbs up and kept walking. The beach was too beautiful and I was too relaxed to get upset. Dogs ran around chasing tennis balls in the water, children were building sandcastles and old ladies enjoyed the water sitting on beach chairs, in the sea. This was the place to be.

After a few more near misses with the Frisbee, I started ducking automatically every time I heard 'whizzzz' nearby. Everyone seemed to be enjoying the happy chaos that reigned on this beach. Well, except the poor lifeguard who was still trying to stop people swimming and still being ignored. It was all part of the atmosphere and I loved it.

"OH NO!"

"What's wrong?" Emily called out form her room where she was packing her suitcase.

"My skirts are still wet. I thought they would be dry by

now, but they're very damp. I can't pack them in the suitcase like this."

Emily walked into my room with her hairdryer. "Here, use this. It's more humid here than Jerusalem, so they probably won't dry well on their own."

I took the hairdryer and plugged it in with a sigh. "Looks like I'll be up for a while."

Emily cringed. "Need help? I can use the small hotel hair dryer on the other skirt."

"No, it's ok. You go to sleep, I'll just dry them enough so I can pack them in the suitcase tomorrow morning."

"Are you sure?"

"Yes. Goodnight." I closed the connecting door after her and draped the skirt over the back of a chair. At least I had an old Bollywood movie playing in the background for entertainment while I blow dried my skirts.

As tired as I was, I didn't fall asleep right away. I kept thinking about the differences between the two cities. Staying in Jerusalem was almost like stepping back in time, but Tel Aviv felt like a completely different country. I hadn't seen any children working in Tel Aviv, and people didn't walk around with a look of survival in their eyes. It was new, it was modern, and the only armed soldiers I had seen were the girls with pink handbags at the market. It felt familiar and comforting, as though I had returned home to Melbourne.

CHAPTER 8
TYPICAL TOURIST EXPERIENCES

The elevator doors opened and the first thing I saw was a group of people huddled around a tall, slim woman wearing a cowboy hat.

"Tour of Israel?" she said with a light European accent I didn't recognise.

"Yes, this is our booking," Emily told her, handing over our tickets.

The woman checked our names and turned to the small group in front of her; the Canadian couple I had met at breakfast, an elderly couple with a strong English accent, a tall and very thin middle aged man with an equally tall and thin older version of himself, and a slim woman with two bored teenagers.

"Good morning, group," the woman in the cowboy hat addressed us in the brisk tone of a school principal. "I am your tour guide, Julia. We have a busy day so we better start. Get your luggage outside to the bus and the driver Mahmud will put it in storage."

"Is that all of us then, love?" the English man said in an accent that reminded me of Jamie Oliver. Almost twice the height of his wife, he was well rounded with a fair, slightly sunburnt, complexion and very white hair.

"No, Mr… " Julia paused to check his name from her list.

"Just call me Humphry, love. And this here is me missus, Ethel." He pointed his thumb to the small woman with a straw blond bob and thick glasses standing next to him.

"Thank you Humphry. The other group members are staying in other hotels nearby. We will pick them up on our way to Masada. Hurry up please, we don't want to keep Mahmud waiting or he will be grumpy."

Like obedient schoolchildren, we grabbed our luggage and hurriedly followed her outside where a short, dark skinned man with a military haircut started grabbing suitcases and throwing them into the storage area under the bus.

When his hairy hand reached for my suitcase I held on firmly.

"Please be careful, fragile," I said in Arabic. My experiences in Israel so far had taught me that the locals take you more seriously if you try to speak in their language.

He stared at me in surprise. "Inti btihki Arabi? *(You speak Arabic?)*"

"Shway *(A little)*. Beenkisir *(Fragile)*," I repeated, pointing to my suitcase.

"Shoo ismik? *(What is your name?)*"

"Noor."

"You are Arabic? You no look Arabic."

I switched back to English because it was easier. "My mum's Lebanese and my dad is Italian," I explained.

If I had a dollar for every time I had to explain my parentage and my name to people, I could quit my job and retire immediately.

"Ah! Very nice." He snatched my suitcase and placed it more gently in the bus. "You no worry, I be careful."

"Thank you. And this one too, please," I pointed Emily's suitcase. "We bought a lot of Armenian ceramics in Jerusalem."

"Beautiful," he nodded approvingly. "Yes, yes. You no worry, I take care of it."

I tried not to cringe as he threw in more suitcases and joined Emily on the bus.

"Noor, this is Valeria," Emily introduced the slim, tanned woman with black hair. "And her children Sophie and Mark." She pointed to the two blond teenagers. "Valeria is Italian and her children are half Italian like you, and half Belgian."

I smiled politely. "Nice to meet you."

All three shared the same facial bone structures and slim body shape, but the children's skin, hair and eye colouring was very different. It was the same in my family, with my mum having a darker skin tone than me and my sister.

"This is Peter and his uncle Jack," Emily continued the introductions and I nodded at the tall, thin man and the older looking version of him. "Humphry and Ethel, from the UK but living in Canada," Emily gestured to the older English couple, "Svetlana and Rick, also from Canada. I think you met them at breakfast."

I smiled and waved hello to everyone just as Mahmud turned the engine on and we lurched forward. The bus stopped at four different hotels to pick up the rest of the tour group which included a large and cheerful group of South Africans, an Australian father and son, an older American woman with a southern accent, a middle-aged woman from New York and a New Zealand couple.

Tap, tap, tap.

The loud conversations stopped and heads swivelled towards the front of the bus where Julia was standing with a microphone.

"Welcome. I am your tour guide, Julia, and this is the driver Mahmud. We have a very busy schedule, so please be on time every morning because we have to pick up the members of the group from different hotels. If you are late, Mahmud *will* leave without you and you will have to make your own way to the next stop."

I turned to Emily with raised eyebrows. "I hope she's joking," I whispered.

Julia pulled down a large map of Israel and pointed to a spot that I couldn't read. "This morning we are going to Masada so I will tell you a little bit about it. The fortress is on the edge of the Judean desert, 20 kilometres from the Dead Sea, and it is famous for a sad story." She paused her history lesson for dramatic effect. "A group of Jewish rebels took control of the fortress, and when the Romans finally ended the siege, they found them dead. Rather than be captured, 960 rebels killed their wives and children before committing suicide."

A collective gasp of horror came from the group.

"It is a very interesting place. Even though we are in the desert, the fortress was well built with an aqua-duct system that provided fresh water. We will go up the fortress in a cable car and watch a short movie before walking around the ruins. Please stay together and take hats. It is very hot in Masada."

Hot was an understatement; it was like stepping into a furnace. The sun beat down on us mercilessly and there was little shade among the ruins. Here, on top of the rocky plateau, we were completely exposed to the elements and it seemed impossible to me that people could have lived in these conditions. The local tour guide was giving us detailed explanations of the fortress, taking us from place to place but the older members of our tour group soon started lagging behind, red faced and panting.

"Come along dear, you're falling behind again," Ethel called out to Humphry as he took another photo with his iPad.

The guide had stopped to explain something else and I took the opportunity to move closer to the edge of the fortress. The view was breathtaking. The emptiness of the Judean desert stretched for miles, nothing but sky and sand, and the howling wind in my ears.

"If you need to use the bathroom, please be quick because Mahmud is waiting. Next stop is Dead Sea," Julia announced.

And just like that, the magic of the desert was shattered.

"Do we have time to buy souvenirs?" the American woman with the southern accent asked.

"Well, we don't have much time Ms, um ... "

"Jean. So we won't have time to buy souvenirs?"

"What souvenirs do you need?" Julia frowned.

"I don't know, a keychain for my son or something. Do they take American dollars? I only have American dollars."

"Yeah, what's the rush? We're on holiday," the younger American woman joined in. "I want to buy souvenirs too."

Julia sighed. "Alright, alright. Everyone, we will stop for 10 minutes for bathroom break and you can buy souvenirs from gift shop if you like. But I am telling you, they are cheap quality souvenirs and not made in Israel."

The group hurried inside while Julia yelled after them "Only 10 minutes! 10 Minutes! Mahmud is waiting!"

I lingered for a last look and photo of the magnificent desert, before hurriedly using the bathrooms and rushing onto the bus. I was fairly certain she had been joking about the driver leaving stragglers behind, but I didn't want to risk it. Just in case.

THE CLOSER WE got to the Dead Sea, the hotter it became. I wasn't the only one suffering from the heat but luckily for my travel companions, Mahmud came to the rescue. As well as being a bus driver, he ran a side business selling small water bottles to tourists for 4 shekels each. Emily and I were the only ones who didn't buy from him, being well organised with our own supply of 1.5 L bottles from the Old City for five shekels each.

"You must all be hungry, so we will stop for quick lunch before continuing to Dead Sea," Julia said to cheers from the crowd.

I was very hungry, and the continental breakfast I had enjoyed in the morning seemed like a lifetime ago.

Emily was looking out the window with a dubious expression. "Where are they taking us for lunch? There is nothing around here other than rocks and Bedouin tents and goats."

"I would love to eat with Bedouins," I said, getting my hopes up only to have them dashed as the bus stopped by a dingy looking petrol station / café.

"I really hope they have a vegan option," Emily mumbled.

"You should be more worried that they will have anything edible," I muttered darkly.

"Maybe it looks worse than it is," Emily tried to be optimistic, but I doubted it.

The inside was passably clean and setup like a school cafeteria; where we all had to line up with our own tray, plate and cutlery, waiting to be served by apathetic lunch ladies.

"Oh, good! I can have rice and long green beans."

I couldn't bring myself to share Emily's enthusiasm as I looked at the greasy rice and beans that had been boiled within an inch of their life. Still, it looked better than the wilted salad bits, soggy spaghetti and sand paper dry schnitzel. Cringing, I ordered some rice, green beans and a piece of oily chicken.

"Well, at least it will be cheap," I told Emily.

"After 5% discount, 47 shekels," the cashier told me.

"Sorry?"

"47 shekels," she repeated in a bored tone.

My mouth opened and closed a few times before I handed over the money and followed Emily to an empty table.

"I don't think I can have any more." I pushed the plate away from me and stood.

"Lucky for us, we have nuts and fruit in our backpack. We can eat that on the bus."

"That was truly the most disgusting food I have ever eaten. Even the food covered in flies in the Old City can't be worse than this," I grumbled to Emily as we climbed into the bus.

"Here, have a nut bar," she offered. "Forget lunch, we're going to the Dead Sea!"

I smiled. "Good thing we have that to look forward to."

THE BUS AIR conditioner was turned on at full blast, but it made little difference. I, like many others, had resorted to fanning myself with my tour itinerary papers. The only ones who seemed un-phased by the heat were Mahmud and Julia. Probably because they were sitting right under the air conditioner.

"Before we go to the Dead Sea, we will stop at a factory where they make the famous Dead Sea products, to learn how they are made," Julia announced into her microphone.

I looked at Emily and rolled my eyes. "I bet they will try to make us buy things."

Emily laughed. "Of course they will. I might buy some if it's not too expensive, but if it is, I'll just buy it from the airport in Jordan. It was quite cheap there."

"You don't need to wait until we fly out from Jordan. They sell them everywhere in the Old City for bargain prices."

The bus pulled into a large and empty parking lot and we all filed inside to sit on hard plastic chairs in front of a large projector.

A chubby old woman in a white lab coat stood in front of the group and signalled for silence. "Welcome. This factory makes authentic Dead Sea products that are famous all over the world. You will watch a short video showing you how it is made and the wonderful properties it has. There are many cheap and fake imitations, but our products are the best quality. They do amazing things for your skin, as you will see in the video."

The lights dimmed and the propaganda movie started playing. A beautiful, young Israeli model appeared on the screen, slathering her already glowing skin with the rich, black Dead Sea mud while a voice lectured about the practically miraculous benefits of the minerals.

"I'd be more impressed and buy some if they showed the

wrinkles disappear from an old woman's face," I muttered to Emily who stifled a giggle.

The lights turned on again and Julia stood in front of the group. "The lady will take you into the showroom where you can try products and buy some if you like."

The women in the group rushed to try on products, but I held back and tried not to show much interest in case it attracted the attention of one of the sales girls hovering around.

Emily gasped and almost dropped the container she was holding. "Guess how much this foot cream is?"

"50 shekels?"

"1,080 shekels, which is approximately 300 AUD."

"You can't be serious," I told her with a laugh and took the container to look at the price tag. I blinked and rubbed my eyes, just to be sure I wasn't seeing things. "I can't believe it. $300 for a foot cream!"

"You like?" A young salesgirl asked from behind. "We give discount and make 1060 shekels. Is the best foot product, not cheap imitation."

Very carefully, I put the container back on the shelf and started moving towards the exit. "I'm fine, thank you."

"Me too," Emily quickly added, following me towards the bus before any more sales girls could try to pressure us into buying.

"I thought it would be cheaper here, especially from the factory where they make it, but it's the same price as the ones they sell in Australia," I told Emily.

We weren't the first people on the bus and within minutes, the rest of the group had followed us. According to the group's gossip, only two people bought from there, and none of them were Australians or English. Apparently, we shared a love of bargains as well as a common system of Government among the Commonwealth.

. . .

THE HEAT WORSENED as the bus moved closer to the Dead Sea. I opened another bottle of water, thanking my lucky stars I had stocked up in the Old City or I would have been broke by now if I had to keep buying from Mahmud.

After we all lined up to rent towels at the entrance office, and put on our bathers in the change rooms, we negotiated our way down a very rocky, steep hill descending into the sea.

Don't slip, don't slip, don't slip! One wrong move and I would be rolling all the way down.

Other busloads of tourists were already there, covering their pasty European bodies with black mud from the sea.

"What do we do first? Go in the water or put on the miraculous mud Julia told us about?"

"Go into the water, I guess. But don't take pictures of me as I try to get in!" Emily ordered.

"Oh come on! That's half the fun. I want photos of me posing in the water," I told her as I began wading in, only to flop onto my stomach in an undignified manner.

Laughter erupted from my tour companions while I splashed and tried to push my feet down to stand up.

"Help me," I laughed as Emily gracefully floated past. "I can't stand up. The water keeps pushing my legs up!"

"You can't stand up, there's too much salt in the water. Turn over and float."

Easier said than done. It was the most bizarre feeling of no gravity and being unable to control your body. Trying to stand in the shallow water was almost impossible because the water pushed against my legs and lifted them before I knew what was happening.

"Aaaah! It burns!" I pulled my feet out of the water and floated on my back with my legs in the air like an overturned tortoise.

"Oh no, you poor thing! Is it your blister?" Emily asked.

"Yes! I can't believe how much it burns!"

"Want a picture, girls?" Humphry offered. "The missus is on the sand, she can take some."

I looked over at Ethel who waved and held up her husband's iPad.

"Thanks Humphry," Emily said with a smile.

"Cheers!" I tried to look cool and relaxed for the camera, floating on my back with my sunglasses on, and it was going well until my thongs slipped off my feet and slowly floated away from me.

"Emily, quick, catch my thong – it's next to your elbow!"

"Oh my God! Your *thong* came off?" Jean asked with a shocked look on her face.

"She means flip-flops," said the younger American woman next to her.

I was trying to paddle my way to one of them but it was like a bad dream. Every inch I managed to move forward, so did my thong.

"Here, I've got it." The American woman grabbed it from the water and floated over to me.

"Thank you so much!"

"I'm Tiffany. We're on the same tour."

"Nice to meet you, and thanks again," I grinned.

I wanted to stay longer in the water, but the Sun was burning my scalp. Firmly clutching the errant shoe in my hand, I practically crawled my way out of the water and walked over to the mud bins.

"Can you make sure my back is covered?" Emily asked as she slathered the thick, black mud onto her arms. "Julia said our skin will feel incredible after the treatment."

"Sure." I reached into the tall, plastic blue bin and scooped a large amount into my palm. "Oh! It doesn't feel muddy at all. It's more like clay."

"Here, I'll do your back," Emily offered.

I covered every inch of me in the refreshing, and surprisingly cool, mud. It felt wonderful against my hot skin, protecting me from the scorching heat of the sun.

"It's so hot here," Emily complained. "I'm going to wash the mud off and go have a shower. I'll see you on the bus."

"Okay," I waved cheerfully and walked over to Ethel and Humphry who were trying to take a selfie. "Want me to take a photo for you?"

"Can you take one of me too?" Tiffany asked.

"And me," Jean added.

"Sure, no problem."

By the time I had finished taking photos, my skin felt stretched and tight under the mud, which was now dry and cracking.

"Almost time to leave." Julia's voice reached us from above.

I hurried to the open showers, which were many tubes of water attached to shower heads where all the tourists huddled together underneath, with nothing between them for privacy apart from the bathers they were wearing. Avoiding eye contact with the strangers near me, I stepped under a shower head.

This is so awkward! I mean, what do I do? Should I make polite chit-chat? Maybe not, they might think I'm weird, talking to them while they shower.

I washed off most of the mud and trudged up the hill, which seemed to have grown in size since I had walked down not long ago.

Almost there, don't give up, I lied to myself as my feet struggled to move my overheated body forward. The heat haze made the change room seem like a desert mirage.

"Hurry, almost time to leave. 10 minutes!" Julia's voice came from somewhere at the top of the hill. "Mahmud will not wait for late comers."

The threat of being abandoned in a place with a heat that made hell proud was enough to give my legs strength. Valeria and Jean were coming out of the change room so I ran inside and had a quick shower with tepid water, even though I had only opened the cold water tap.

Julia was standing in front of the bus. "Hurry, hurry. Mahmud is leaving," she smiled.

I didn't know if she was joking or not, but I wasn't about to risk it. Apparently neither were Peter and his uncle Jack, who started running from the men's changing room.

"Everyone here?" Julia peered over her sunglasses. "Good. Now, we go to Jerusalem. Not all of you are staying at same hotel, so when Mahmud stops in front of hotel, I will call your names. Mahmud will open the boot and give you your suitcases. Free time this afternoon, tomorrow morning be ready by 8."

THE BUS STOPPED in front of an elegant hotel and Mahmud jumped out, while the engine was still running, to place suitcases on the pavement.

"Emily, Noor, Humphry and Ethel, Valeria and children, you are all staying here," Julia called out from the front of the bus. "Please hurry, we have to drop off the others."

I scrambled out of my seat and followed my travel companions to the reception desk where Julia helped us check in and left as soon as possible. The others in the group left for their rooms so Emily and I decided to enjoy the hotel's rooftop pool before dinner.

The elevator doors opened and I gasped. I could see the entire Old City illuminated by the afternoon sun like a pretty postcard. "Damn," I muttered. "Where is my camera when I need it?"

"This is incredible!" Emily gushed. "The pool is twice as large as the one in Tel Aviv. And they have lounge chairs for sunbathing. I could happily spend all afternoon here."

"Fine by me," I told her. "All that walking around in a group, getting on and off buses, and the hideous heat has left me exhausted."

It was a wonderfully relaxing afternoon but we didn't stay in the pool for long. Although the view was spectacular, the water was cold and there was a cool breeze that sent us inside to enjoy the opulent lounge.

"What should we do about dinner?" Emily asked. "We are close to the Old City, but if you're tired we could eat here in the hotel restaurant."

I was listening to the pianist with my eyes half closed, my fingers drumming the classical tune on the plush armrest. "Mmmm? Um, sure. As long as it's not too expensive."

"How expensive can a falafel wrap be?" Laughing, she picked up a menu from the coffee table and gasped. "43 shekels!"

"What is?"

"A falafel wrap, with cucumber, tomato, tahini and pita bread. 43 shekels."

I reached over and plucked the menu from her hand. "I can't believe this. It's double the price of what we were charged in Tel Aviv."

"Did you see the other prices on the list? The only thing we can afford to eat here is the breakfast, which thankfully is included in the booking."

I nodded. "Fancy a walk to the Old City for dinner?"

"I thought you were tired?"

"Not tired enough to eat here. Besides, we can restock our water supply and snacks."

Emily nodded and we left quickly before the waiters made their way over to take our order.

THE COURTYARD outside the Damascus Gate was noisy and crowded. I grinned. It was familiar and I had missed the colourful chaos of this enchanting city. We bought our 6 shekel falafel wraps with chips and a drink, and sat on the steps outside the Damascus Gate.

I loved this time of the day, when day and night begin to merge and life in Jerusalem slows down to savour the moment. Young boys sat on top of the stone wall and flew their kites as high as they would go. It seemed to be a fierce competition, and I munched on my falafel, happily watching my favourite kite swirl high above me.

The fruit and vegetable vendors were shouting their prices, one more loudly than the others. I had seen this young boy selling fruit before. Thin and tanned, as though he lived in sunshine all day, he looked around 10 or 11 years old. My eyes flicked back and forth between his shop, a blanket on the ground where he had laid boxes of fruit, and the boys playing with their kites. Although his dark brown eyes occasionally looked towards the other boys playing, his focus was on potential customers.

"Emily, look at that." I indicated towards him with my head. "He should be playing with the other children, not working."

"It's so sad. What's he selling?"

I tilted my head to get a better look. "Apricots, grapes and bananas. They look pretty ripe, even from here."

"We could buy some from him," Emily suggested and I nodded.

"We'll probably have to throw them out, but at least it will be a sale. He hasn't had any customers the whole time we've been sitting here."

"I'm sure we'll be able to eat some of them."

A thin, old man with long, un-kept grey hair and dirty clothes casually strolled down with a bemused look on his face and sat behind the boy. The boy turned to look at him, but continued to shout his prices.

"Hello Baseem, how are you?" a middle aged man asked the boy.

"I'm good mister. What would you like?"

"Give me some bananas."

I smiled, happy that young Baseem had a sale while I finished my dinner.

The old man sitting behind Baseem pulled out a suspicious looking home-made cigarette and lit it, blowing smoke close to the fruit.

Baseem turned to the old man with a frown and snapped in Arabic. "Zeeh *(Move away)*!"

The man ignored him and continued to puff away.

"Zeeh!" Baseem yelled.

"What's going on?" Emily asked.

"Not sure, but he clearly doesn't like the old man." I collected my rubbish to throw it out and almost dropped it in shock. "What the! Did he just - ?" I turned to Emily with wide eyes.

Her jaw was hanging open.

"Should we do something?" I looked around and the local men were looking at the old man and frowning. Some were grumbling and a few shouted at him to move on.

The man had put his hand down his pants and kept it there as he puffed away.

That was the last straw for Baseem. "Isa ma bitzeeh, bishbaak kaffain! *(If you don't move away, I'll give you two slaps!)*," he threatened.

The man ignored him, hand down pants, cigarette in mouth.

SPLAT!

A very ripe apricot landed on the man, not that he seemed to notice or care.

SPLAT, SPLAT, SPLAT!

The barrage of apricots continued until the man stood and walked away.

Peace was restored and we bought two boxes of grapes from the brave young boy. The sun had set and it would be dark soon so we hurried inside the Old City to buy snacks from the local stalls and restock our water supply.

"Hello Jiddo *(grandpa)*," I grinned at the old man who reminded me of my grandpa. "Badna nishtri mayhe *(we want to buy water)*."

He gave us a big, and almost toothless smile, and sold us eight large water bottles for 20 shekels. I explained to Emily in English that he had given us a discount. He usually sold a 1.25 L bottle for five shekels, when other vendors nearby sold it for 8, and this time he was only charging us 2.5 shekels per bottle. When Emily tried to thank him, he waved his hands and smiled.

"Sakri, sakri *(close it, close it)*!" He pointed to my backpack and I tugged the zip closed all the way.

Trying not to drop my water bottles, I waved goodbye awkwardly. *This might be the last time I see him,* I thought sadly. It had been so wonderful to have a friendly face in a country where I was a foreigner and he had always treated us kindly. I knew that when I would reminisce about Jerusalem in the future, I would always remember his little shop and kind smile.

CHAPTER 9
ALL ROADS LEAD TO ROME AND
ALL TOURS GO TO JERUSALEM

Breakfast was a superb buffet of various salads, coleslaw, bagels, pretzels, cheeses, yogurt, stewed fruit, cakes, sardines and other pickled fish, but the most impressive part was the omelette station where the chef prepared your eggs however you wanted. Unfortunately the omelette line was too long, so I sampled almost everything else on offer and headed for our designated pick up point. Still unsure if Julia had been joking about Mahmud not waiting for passengers, Emily and I made sure we were ready and waiting before 8 am.

Our first stop for the day was the Holocaust Museum, a reminder of the cruelty that humans are capable of. The saddest part for me was walking through a long and very dark tunnel, lit only by tiny lights that looked like twinkling stars in the night sky. Each light represented one of the children that died during the Holocaust, and as I walked through, the recorded voice read out each child's name and the age they died. I had learned about the Holocaust in history classes at school, but learning about it and seeing the human hair and personal belongings of the victims brought their suffering to life.

How can people do this to each other? I kept asking myself.

Animals only kill to eat or protect their home and families. If humans are supposedly superior to animals, how can they behave this way? I just couldn't understand why.

It seemed that today's itinerary was more sombre because the next stop was the Mount of Olives and the garden of Gethsemane, some of the holiest sites for Christians. Not that I felt anything spiritual. I couldn't. Not when I was shuffling around in a large group, stopping to take photos of these holy landmarks and places. I really hoped that our visit to Bethlehem would feel less commercial.

I was quiet during the bus ride to Bethlehem. The morning's visit to the Holocaust Museum had left me feeling very sombre and not in the mood for idle chitchat.

"Pay attention everybody," Julia called out from the front of the bus. "We have reached the West Bank military checkpoint. We need to go through it to visit Bethlehem."

"Did she say West Bank?" I asked Emily sharply.

Emily's lips were pressed in a thin line. "I didn't realise Bethlehem was in the West Bank."

Don't panic, don't panic, I told my racing heart. "We ticked that we weren't going to the West Bank on our travel documents." I hissed.

"I know, but it's too late to do anything about it now."

I took several deep breaths. "What if they find out we did while we're leaving Israel, and we get arrested?"

"Calm down, you always jump to the worst conclusion." Emily told me. "We didn't know."

The bus had stopped and the doors opened. Two Israeli soldiers with angry expressions and rifles clasped in their hands climbed on board.

"Please stay in your seats," Julia instructed on her microphone. "Hold up your passports above your head in one hand, and leave the other hand empty on your lap. Please do not move from your seats."

"Well, that doesn't sound intimidating at all," I muttered to Emily.

The soldiers took their time walking down the bus and looking at every passport. No one spoke, and when they finally climbed off a collective sigh of relief echoed through the bus.

"I leave you here and Mahmud will take you through to Bethlehem where you will meet your local tour guide. She is very nice and I am sure you will have a good time."

"Wait a minute," Tiffany called out from her seat somewhere in the middle of the bus. "Why are you leaving us?"

"Because I am Jewish. Your local tour guide is a Palestinian Christian, that is why she will take over your tour in Bethlehem. I will be back later."

"What about lunch? When do we eat?" Humphry called out from the back of the bus.

"Mahmud has organised your lunch and will take you to a restaurant before you start the tour in Bethlehem. If there are no more questions, I will leave now. No questions? Okay, I will see you later."

An unusual silence filled the bus. My shoulders tensed as my eyes took in the massively tall and thick concrete walls that surrounded the city of Bethlehem. It looked more like a fortified prison than a city and I felt trapped.

Mahmud drove the bus to a shabby looking restaurant. "We eat lunch here and meet guide at church."

He climbed off to hug and kiss a middle-aged couple standing outside the restaurant while I reluctantly followed the others inside the empty dining area.

Long rectangular tables were set with small dishes of stale looking hommous with crusty edges and a side-dish of wilted salad.

"Okay, sit. We don't have much time before we have to meet guide. They "- he indicated behind him to the middle-aged couple - "will take your order. You can choose between beef or chicken. 60 shekel each and if you want drink, is extra."

"What?!" Someone called out. "60 shekel each? That's expensive."

Mahmud frowned. "You pay me before food."

"Why can't we go somewhere else?" said Tiffany. "I saw other cafes around here."

"No," Mahmud said sternly. "Lunch has been organised and cooked."

"Yes, but you didn't ask us and this isn't listed as an included lunch on the itinerary. It's optional so we don't have to eat here if we don't want to," a man from the group spoke up.

"I'm not paying 60 shekel and extra for drink when we can't even choose what to eat."

I wanted to turn my head and see who said that but I was watching Mahmud's tanned face turn darker and the vein in his neck throb.

"No go anywhere else. You don't pay, you don't eat."

Several people shrugged, walked away from the set tables and sat at empty ones.

"What should we do?" Emily whispered. "It's very expensive, and I'm not sure they have a vegan option. I don't want to pay 60 shekels for this awful looking hummous and salad."

I nodded and my stomach rumbled. "Me either but I'm not sure I can last until dinnertime. I think I'll just have to pay and eat what I can," I fumed.

"Yes, I'm so hungry that wilted salad is looking good."

Mahmud waved his hands and spoke loudly in Arabic to the middle-aged couple who were glaring at the full table of rebels. Those of us too hungry to skip lunch sat down and chose between the chicken or beef. I didn't want to pay 6 shekels extra for a can of coke so I didn't order a drink.

Thump.

I jumped in my seat as Mahmud's hairy hand plonked down a can of coke in front of me and Emily.

"For you and your friend. Free," he said in Arabic and walked away.

"I thought you weren't going to order a drink?" Emily asked.

"Shhhh! I didn't," I whispered.

Blushing and cringing, I leaned in and quietly told her what happened. The last thing I wanted was for the group members to find out and think that I was getting special treatment. What I really wanted to do was refuse the drink, but that would offend him and I didn't want to risk upsetting him. I didn't trust him not to be vindictive and drive the bus off without me on it.

A plate with a few small pieces of dry, shrivelled up meat landed in front of me. I looked over at the rebels' table wistfully and tried to swallow as much of my expensive lunch as I could. The grumblings from the others at my table made it clear no one else was happy with this prearranged, more like an ambush, lunch.

"FINISH EATING? WE WALK TO CHURCH," Mahmud barked and walked out of the restaurant.

It was a short walk to the Church of the Nativity, but a very interesting one. Bethlehem seemed full of luxurious cars and pro-Palestinian graffiti spray painted all over the concrete walls that surrounded us.

"This is guide," Mahmud pointed to a short woman with dyed blond hair standing in front of a mediaeval looking church, and walked off.

"Hello everybody," she smiled broadly. "I am Christina and I will be your guide in Bethlehem. Welcome. Behind me is the famous Church of the Nativity. Why is it famous? Because it is where Jesus was born. So it is a very special place for Christians. See interesting door?" She pointed to a very small, stone doorway. "Look higher. That is outline of the original door. It was much bigger but they made it smaller so that horses could not go through the doorway. Now we go inside and you can see exactly where Jesus was born, because it is marked with a star on the ground."

I grinned at Emily. Christmas was my favourite time of the year, and my family, like many other Italians, have a strong tradition of setting up elaborate nativity scenes. I was picturing a giant nativity scene inside the grey stone walls of the Church, but my enthusiasm dimmed when I stepped inside.

"Come closer everybody, I have to talk quietly," Christina whispered loudly and a few heads turned in our direction. "This is a very special Church and it belongs to the major Christian denominations. They have their own service at different times of the day, and the priests of course share the altar space."

I looked around with wide eyes.

This is definitely the most bizarre looking Church I have ever seen. It's like a competition, trying to outdo each other with the décor and stake their claim on it.

I didn't know where to look – there were so many orna-ments that instead of looking mystical and holy, I thought it looked tacky.

"Now, over here is the Greek-Orthodox part -" Christina waved her arm at a section that looked like Aladdin's cave. "Of course, it is all real gold," she whispered excitedly.

The flickering candle flames reflected off the shiny gold, forcing me to look away.

Sometimes, less really is more.

I followed the others, taking photos where permitted, and was glad when we were back outside in the sunshine.

"And now, good news," Christina announced with a big smile. "We go souvenir shopping. I take you to a nice place where they make things here in Bethlehem. Mahmud will pick you up from there."

I followed the others into the store and gasped. It was beautiful. It was magnificent. It was full of every nativity scene imaginable, made of the most exquisite, smooth wood. I picked up a basket and started filling it with small statues and nativity sets for all my grandparents, my cousin Amalia, and the rest of my family. Emily had filled her own small basket and we lined up to pay when we saw our bus pull up outside.

A hairy arm leaned on the counter next to me and I looked up to see Mahmud.

"Give them discount," he pointed at me and Emily. "She is half Lebanese," he nodded his head in my direction, winked and walked off.

Heat flooded my face. I hated special treatment and I didn't want to owe him anything. "It's okay, I'll pay the full price," I told the cashier but he shook his head.

"No, no! Friend of Mahmud is my friend. I give you and your friend 10% off."

"Really, you don't have to – "

"No, no problem," he interrupted and smiled. "Our pleasure."

I gritted my teeth and tried to smile. "Thank you."

BEEP, BEEP.

"Is that Mahmud beeping from the bus?" Emily asked, putting away her wallet.

"I think he's telling the group to hurry up. Come on, I don't want to be left behind here. This place feels more like a prison than a city."

"Empty threats. I doubt he would actually leave anyone behind," Emily said with a smile, but I did not share her optimism.

Judging by the queue to climb onto the bus, neither did many of the others.

"Beautiful necklaces, cheap price," yelled a middle aged man hovering near the bus.

Out of the corner of my eye, I could see his arms were covered in long, beaded necklaces. I knew better than to look or show any interest so I stared in front of me and climbed on the bus as soon as I could.

"Cheap beautiful necklace," he dangled them in front of the last members of our tour group waiting to board the bus.

BEEEP.

Mahmud was getting impatient, but there was nothing to be done. Only one person could fit through the door at a time.

I watched my travel companion, a South African woman, shake her head and try to get onto the bus but the vendor would not let her until she bought something.

"Oh no," I muttered to Emily who was peering through the window with me. "She's trying to haggle for the price. She'll never get away now."

BEEEEEEEEP.

"I am leaving. Get on or stay here," Mahmud barked out of the door.

Someone gasped.

"He wouldn't dare! Would he?"

"Quick, just buy it and get on!" someone shouted.

The woman paid for a necklace and tried to walk away, but the vendor was determined to sell more. He pulled off the other necklaces from his arm and started shouting.

"Special price, big bargain. Buy them all for special price!"

The woman shook her head and tried to move around him but he blocked her.

"Just buy it!" someone else shouted. "Hurry!"

BEEEEEEEP.

Eyes wide and looking slightly alarmed, the woman handed over money to the vendor and climbed the bus, clutching a bunch of necklaces.

The doors shut immediately and Mahmud took off.

I stared at the driver's seat with my mouth open.

"I can't believe he didn't intervene!" I whispered to Emily.

She shook her head, her lips pressed in a grim line.

"That's not right," Tiffany said from her seat behind us. "I'm telling Julia what he did."

"Yeah, and I'm telling her about the lunch he organised,"

Jean added. "It was disgusting and we had to pay 60 shekels for it!"

"We should have gotten a choice," Humphries grumbled from his seat across the aisle.

Peter and his Uncle Jack nodded.

I leaned back in my seat. It seemed I wasn't the only one not impressed with our driver's behaviour. Tonight's program was an optional excursion to the Old City, but Emily and I had decided to go on our own so I wouldn't have to put up with his bad temper for a few hours.

"HELLO GIRLS," Ethel waved as they came closer. "It's so nice of you to take us on a night tour of the Old City."

"I can't wait to see it after everything you've told me." Humphries held up his iPad with a mischievous grin.

"We'll have to keep an eye on him in the crowd so he doesn't get lost," Ethel told us. "The problem is, he gets so excited and stops to take pictures – then he disappears in the crowd!"

I laughed and slid on my backpack. "Don't worry Ethel, we'll make sure he doesn't get lost."

The first thing we did was buy a falafel wrap for dinner from our favourite store. I couldn't tell what Humphries enjoyed more, the actual food or the price. Our next stop was the market in the lane where we had stayed for four days.

"Oh my! Look at all those lovely sweets! Shall we try some, Humphry?" Ethel looked over her shoulder. "Humphry?"

I looked beside me where he had been standing a moment ago. "Damn! He's gone again. Emily," I yelled over the noise of the crowd, hoping she would hear me from where she was standing two stalls further down.

Emily turned towards us with raised eyebrows. "Humphry?" she yelled back and I nodded.

I scanned the crowd for Humphry's white hair and striped

polo shirt. "Found him!" I yelled and pointed in the direction we had come from.

Happily oblivious of the concern he had caused his wife, Humphry was taking photos of the big spice pyramid on his iPad.

"Truck!" Emily and I yelled simultaneously.

Humphry jumped and scrambled to press his body against the store front to avoid being run over. The people around him jammed themselves in every crevice they could find to avoid the small truck's tyres, and calmly returned to their shopping when it had passed.

Humphry walked over to us with a big smile. "Well, that was close. Lucky I'm getting better at jumping out of the way."

I frowned. There was an unusual amount of motor traffic tonight. For whatever reason, small trucks and cars kept trying to squeeze through the lanes, forcing people to climb over each other and cram in the small stores to avoid being hit.

"Let's take them to look at the sunset at the Western wall," I told Emily.

Keeping a close eye on Humphry, we wove our way through the crowded lanes towards the Western Wall and Dome of the Rock.

"Goodness, what are all these little candles for?" Ethel asked.

I looked down at the tea light candles in brown paper bags filled with sand. There was a path of them leading to the viewpoint of the Western Wall, all lit as though guiding our way.

"No idea. We're very close and I think we'll make it in time to see the sunset," I told them.

I took them the same way the local tour guide had shown us days ago.

"Here it – what's this?"

"Oh, isn't it beautiful!" Ethel exclaimed and Humphry

began snapping photos.

Emily grimaced. "Ooops. I think we've walked in on a wedding."

I eyed the red carpet leading to the small table covered in white cloth, the wedding cake, champagne bottle and glasses. "Lucky for us the bridal party wasn't here or we would have ruined their photo shoot."

"Gosh, look at that sunset," Ethel said, her eyes wide.

It was glorious. No wonder the wedding couple wanted to take their photos here.

"We should probably go before they arrive," Emily said.

"Let's go somewhere and get a cool drink. My treat!" Humphry grinned.

"Cheers," I grinned back.

There was only one café I knew of with outdoor tables and chairs, so we took them back to the Via Dolorosa where we had eaten our tiny, overpriced pizza.

THE CAFÉ WAS full of people, like it had been every time I had walked past. This time though, it was mostly full of local men. We ordered our drinks and sat outside to relax and enjoy the evening breeze.

"We should leave soon, before it gets too dark," Humphry suggested.

A group of men got up from the table and rushed to the front of the café, talking rapidly and pointing to something small on the ground.

"What's going on?" Ethel asked curiously.

I stopped sipping my minty lemonade and listened to the excited chatter.

"I think - " I stopped and looked at Emily. She adored cats and I wasn't sure how to tell her. "I think they're saying that a kitten fell from the roof."

"What?! Oh my God! Is it ok?"

"Shhh," I held up a finger to my lips and continued eavesdropping. Some of the men were looking up at the roof and pointing. I heard a cat yowl and cringed. My twelve year old cat Susu had never made such a distressed sound.

It must be the mother calling for her kitten. My heart ached. There was no way the kitten could have survived the impact when it hit the ground.

Miaow, miaow.

I jumped out of my seat, my eyes wide and heart racing. "It's alive! I can't believe it – it's alive. Can you hear its mother calling for it?"

Miiiiiiaaaaaaoowwww.

The mother cat had heard her kitten's reply and was calling out desperately.

"Oh dear! Oh, how awful!" Ethel stood from her chair, clutching her wrinkled hands.

One of the men bent down and picked up the kitten by the scruff of the neck.

I breathed a sigh of relief. The locals would help the poor kitten, maybe take it to a vet.

THUMP.

I yelped in shock.

The man had thrown the kitten against the rubbish dumpsters across the road.

If the impact from the roof fall didn't kill it, this surely did!

"Did he – did he just - ? Oh my God."

I turned to look at Emily who had turned an alarming shade of white.

"It's all right dear," Ethel tried to sooth her, patting her arm. "It could have survived. Let's go have a look. It could be ok, don't panic."

The four of us raced to the other side of the road. It was dark, and the street was dimly lit.

"I can't see anything," I complained.

Humphry turned on his iPad and pointed the glowing screen onto the rubbish bags.

"I can hear it," Emily squealed. "It's alive!"

We immediately fell silent and sure enough, a faint meowling was coming from behind the rubbish bins. Now that we knew it was alive, we were determined to reunite the kitten with its mother who was still miaowing and anxiously pacing back and forth on the roof. Our rescue operation had turned into a game of hide and seek. Every time we moved the bins and rubbish bags, the kitten hissed and hid behind something else. After a few well aimed scratches at my hand, I finally managed to pick it up and looked up to find a group of local children staring at us.

The little girl stepped forward and stroked the kitten's head. "Haram *(poor thing)*", she said in a soft voice. "Haram."

The kitten hissed, but I held it securely in my hands so it wouldn't scratch the little girl.

"Trikia, wisih *(leave it, it's dirty)*. Killa maleni amrad *(it's full of diseases)*," the little boys called out and the little girl stepped back.

I smiled at her and moved towards the café to ask the owner for help. Maybe he had a ladder I could borrow? The mother cat was prowling on the roof of the café, staring down at me and her kitten. I sensed the others come stand behind me as I tried to convince the owner that the kitten had to be reunited with its mother. Apart from a few nods and apathetic shrugs, he didn't move.

"Dafayu? *(have they paid?)*" One of the customers called out in Arabic.

The owner looked over his shoulder and nodded.

"Lakehn trikon. Yustuflu. *(Rough translation - In that case, ignore them)*."

The owner looked at me, shrugged and walked into the café.

"What's happening? Isn't he going to help?" Emily demanded.

I shook my head. "We're on our own. Let's find a way to lift the kitten up to the roof. Maybe on the side of the building?"

Humphry held his iPad high so we could see. Luckily for the kitten, there was a tube down the side of the building. I handed the kitten to Emily and lifted my skirts to try and climb high enough to place the kitten on the roof.

"Ok, ok," a man's voice called out. "Ana bitlah *(I will go up.)*"

I turned to look. A middle aged man with a thin build and kind face had followed us into the narrow alleyway. "Ana bitlah," he repeated and pointed to himself.

"What's he saying?" Ethel asked.

"I think he's volunteering to go up," I translated, unable to hide the surprise in my voice.

The man climbed up a few feet and reached down for the kitten. I placed it gently in his hand and watched him anxiously, worried he was going to throw it over onto the roof. Very gently, he placed the kitten on the roof and climbed down.

I let out the breath I hadn't realised I was holding. "Shukran! Shukran! *(Thank you)*."

"Thank you, thank you so much for helping," Emily told him.

"Yes, thank you," Ethel echoed.

The man nodded once and walked away. We moved to the front of the building where the light from the café illuminated parts of the roof. The mother cat raced to where we had deposited the kitten, sniffed it, picked it up by the scruff of the neck and carried it back to the rest of the litter.

I sighed in relief. "I was afraid she might reject it because it was touched by humans," I mumbled, my knees feeling a little wobbly.

"What a night! You girls promised us an adventure in the Old City and you sure delivered!" Humphry laughed heartily.

I smiled weakly. Things were never boring in the Old City.

CHAPTER 10
PILGRIMS

"Hello handsome!"

My head snapped towards Emily. "Who are you talking to?"

Laughing, Emily pointed to the sleek black cat butting his head against her legs.

I knelt down and held out my hand for him to sniff. Very charmingly, he put a paw on my arm and miaowed. My heart melted and like every time I saw a cat or dog in this land, I missed my own fur-kids terribly.

"He's much cleaner than the other cats we saw in the Muslim quarter of the Old City," I commented to Emily.

"Better fed too by the looks of him." She scratched behind his ears and he purred his thanks.

"Mister Humphry, I can see your white knees." Julia's voice floated to the back of the group. "I can't believe so many of you men forgot to wear pants."

"It's too hot to wear long pants," someone grumbled.

"Well, you will have to wear a scarf and cover your knees," Julia said in a no-nonsense tone. "The Western wall is a very holy site for Jewish people and everyone must be dressed modestly. The women all remembered to wear long skirts or pants and long sleeved tops. Why are some of the men dressed inappropriately? Because men never listen."

I, and every other woman in the group, burst out laughing.

"Lucky for you, the Jewish guards at the Western wall let you borrow scarves to cover your knees but you have to return them when we leave. Unfortunately for you, when we go to the Dome of the Rock, you will have to buy a scarf or you won't be allowed to go in. Maybe next time when I give you instructions, you will listen and remember."

"Yes madam!" Humphry saluted and the men sniggered like naughty schoolboys.

Julia shook her head, but couldn't quite hide her smile.

"We should have read the tour itinerary carefully and just come here with the group, instead of spending days trying to find the Dome of the Rock on our own." I shuffled forward in the queue.

"But then we would have missed out on all the fun of trying to find it," Emily pointed out, patting the black cat who was following our progression towards the Western wall.

"Okay, pay attention everyone," Julia's voice commanded. "We're almost at the wall now and we will be separated; Men to the left, women to the right. Please stay in your correct area."

Standing towards the back of the group, I had no hope of seeing over people's heads so I leaned to my side to see what Julia was talking about. A wooden partition was standing between men and women. Many were praying devoutly, tapping books on their forehead, bowing repeatedly, their lips and all their prayers jumbled together into a humming sound.

"Over here is a fountain where you can wash your hands," Julia pointed in front of her. "Before you reach the wall, it is customary to wash your hands in the small fountain, and when you leave – please remember to walk backwards. It is sign of respect in a very holy place. If you like, you can write down a wish or a prayer on a small piece of paper, fold it up and put it in the cracks of the wall. They say that if you pray at this wall, your prayers will be answered. We meet here in 10 minutes."

The women's section was full of chairs, with some women studying religious texts while others prayed or lined up to touch the wall. I washed my hands and lined up in the informal queue, clenching the little scrap of paper with my prayer scribbled on it. The line moved slowly. No one was in a hurry here. Everyday life was on pause while we contemplated more spiritual matters. It was peaceful and comforting.

It was my turn to walk up to the wall, so I copied the women before me and touched my forehead and palm to the cool stone as I wedged my prayer in a gap, among so many others. Very slowly and carefully, I walked backwards.

Please don't let me trip on a chair, I begged the higher powers. *I don't want to be the one to upset the tranquillity here.*

Most of the group was standing with Julia when I arrived, and the men had returned their scarves to the Jewish guards.

Julia motioned with her hands for us to lean in. "Now," she said in a low voice, "we go to Dome of the Rock. They have religious authority who check everyone dressed modestly. You Humphry, and other men showing knees, will have to cover them with scarf." Julia eyed their pasty white knees with a grim expression and Humphry rolled his eyes.

No one escaped the inspection. We all lined up and were examined individually to make sure we were wearing appropriate clothing. Those scandalously baring their knees were marched off in a walk of shame to a room and were relieved of 50 shekels and wrapped in long scarves. Only then were we permitted to continue our tour of the Dome of the Rock.

It was as beautiful as the first time I had seen it, but much more crowded. Besides us there were several other tour groups, and groups of schoolchildren learning the Quran in the glorious sunshine.

"Isn't it beautiful here? And so peaceful."

I snorted, unsuccessfully trying to suppress my laughter.

Emily looked at me with raised eyebrows. "What's so funny? You don't think it's peaceful and beautiful?"

Sniggering, I pointed to the men in our group struggling to hold down their checked pattern cotton scarves. As soon as they pushed the scarf down, another breeze blew it up, revealing glimpses of their pasty white legs.

Emily laughed. "Should have worn pants like Julia told them to."

When we had taken enough photos, Julia led the way down the Via Dolorosa, pointing out the various Stations of the Cross and other interesting sights in the Old City.

"Ouch!" I rubbed my nose. "Sorry," I said to Peter. "I didn't realise you had stopped."

"No problem. I think Julia stopped to show us something."

I stepped out of my place in the back of the group so I could see what Julia was pointing to. It was hard to hear with all the noise around us. *Why on earth has she stopped here? We're in the middle of a market lane.*

"What's she saying?" I asked Emily, but I had a good idea from reading the sign she was pointing to.

Tourists beware
Be careful of people saying they are local tour guides.
They are not licensed tour guides.
When they take you souvenir shopping, they have arrangement with the shop and get a commission.
Shop independently.

"SHE'S TELLING us what we learned when we stayed here," Emily chuckled.

Some of the local shopkeepers were giving Julia a dirty look, which she completely ignored. "Now I take you to the Church of the Holy Sepulchre. As you probably know, it is where Jesus was buried. Inside is the tomb of Christ. If you want to see it, line up and the priest will show you. When we are inside, please speak quietly. This way please."

We walked into a large courtyard crowded with people and school groups of young children, the boys wearing kippas (skull cap head covering) and the little girls wearing headscarves. This was the busiest church we had visited so far.

It was worse inside. Hundreds of people prayed over the stone slab where it is said Christ's body had lain, with grumpy looking priests hovering nearby.

I lined up with the others to walk into the shrine enclosing the tomb of Christ. The priest on duty at the tomb looked eerily like Rasputin, his dark, beady little eyes glaring at tourists.

"In!" He shouted and started moving us into the tomb.

We shuffled forward, bodies crammed together into the small space.

Rasputin priest poked his head in and shouted. "OUT! GET OUT!"

"What? But we just walked in," I muttered to know one in particular.

"GET OUT! NOW!"

Annoyed, I shuffled out after the others who headed straight for Julia to complain about the priest's behaviour. I hate to be a trouble maker but I had to agree with them. It was impossible to treat the place and the situation with the respect it deserves with that kind of behaviour.

Julia's lips pressed into a thin line and her eyes narrowed. I almost felt sorry for the priest when she marched off to complain to his supervisor, but really, he had brought it upon himself.

A very disappointing visit to what is probably the most important church in Christianity.

· · ·

THE REST of the morning was spent in a blur of churches. Each had a name and a story, each significant in their own way, but they blended in my mind.

"And now, something different," Julia announced to our tired group.

We had spent the entire morning walking all over the Old City, and the midday sun was very warm.

"This is our last stop before lunch. It is a very special place for Jews. It is the tomb of the famous King David, and it is said that if you touch the cover of his tomb while you pray, your prayers will be answered. Follow me everyone."

I followed my travel companions closely. In this maze of small residential streets, it would be very easy to get lost. Like some other holy sites, the tomb of the great King David was understated; wooden pews for people to sit on, a wooden banister separating the actual stone tomb from the praying section and bare stone walls. The most luxurious item in there was the embroidered purple cover draped over the tomb.

This is more like it. Less crowded, and a quiet place of reflection as a religious place should be.

When everyone had taken their photos, Julia took us back to the bus. According to my stomach, it was well past lunchtime.

"Is everyone here?" Julia counted our heads from the front of the bus. "Humphry?"

Ethel stood, wringing her hands. "He's not here. I thought he was at the back of the group."

"Has anyone seen Humphry?" Julia asked.

The bus erupted with excited chatter.

"Who saw him last?"

"I thought I saw him walking to the bus with us... or was that from the bus?"

"He was taking pictures at the tomb of David."

"I haven't seen him since the tomb of David."

Poor Ethel stood with a pained expression, wringing her

hands. "Oh dear, I keep telling him not to stray. He just gets so distracted taking pictures … "

Mahmud and Julia were engaged in a heated discussion. Her frown and his surly expression were not a good omen.

Julia marched down the aisle and spoke gently to Ethel. "Mahmud says he cannot park here and we have to leave. Do you think Mr Humphry will be able to get back to the hotel?"

"Oh dear… I suppose so."

"I am sorry, we have no idea where he is and we can't keep the bus here until we find him."

"I can go look for him," Peter volunteered.

Julia shook her head. "No, you might get lost too."

"I won't go too far, I'll just retrace our steps some of the way and see if he is there. I remember the way to the bus, I'll be fine."

Ethel's eyes lit up behind her thick glasses. "Oh would you dear?"

"Well," Julia hesitated. "If you are sure you won't get lost. I can only give you five minutes and then Mahmud will drive off. I don't want to lose another member."

"It's okay, I can always catch a taxi back to the hotel," Peter reassured her.

His uncle Jack stood up. "I can help you look for him."

"I'll be fine. I'll be right back."

Without wasting any more time, Peter got off the bus and ran back the way we had come. While he looked for Humphry, Emily and I took turns trying to keep Ethel calm.

"They can't be serious about leaving without Humphry," I whispered to Emily. "I mean, he's an old man in a foreign city and he doesn't know the language. We don't even know if he remembers the name of the hotel we're staying at."

"I really hope Peter finds him. Mahmud looks determined to leave."

I cringed and looked out the window. "There's Peter!"

"Is Humphry with him?" Ethel asked anxiously.

I shook my head. Peter had finished reporting to Julia and walked back to his seat near ours.

"I'm sorry Ethel, I couldn't find him anywhere. I went back to the tomb of David but he wasn't in there and I didn't see him on the way back to the bus."

"It's alright dear, thank you for trying. I'm sure he's fine. He must be taking pictures somewhere and doesn't even realise we've left the tomb."

The bus moved forward.

I gasped. "We're not really leaving are we?"

Ethel's lips were pressed together, her hands clutching each other. "I'm sure he'll be fine. He'll meet us back at the hotel."

Emily looked at me, worry clear in her eyes.

I snapped my mouth shut. Ethel was trying to be brave and I didn't want to worry her, but I couldn't help feeling worried. And appalled. And angry.

Julia walked over to Ethel's seat in front of ours. "I'm sorry Ethel. We could not wait anymore. We'll have lunch and go to museum as planned, and I'm sure Humphry will be at the hotel when we get there in the afternoon."

"Yes… well… yes, alright. I'm sorry to have caused so much trouble. I'm sure he'll be fine."

"Yes, of course. I will go call the hotel and tell them to keep an eye out for him," Julia said in a reassuring tone and returned to her seat.

I ground my teeth together. *Should I say something to Julia? Demand that Mahmud stop the bus? We can start a search party and look for him. But then, what if more people get lost? But we can't just leave him here alone! He's an old man! What if he has heat stroke and is lying unconscious somewhere? I should get off and look for him – who am I kidding? With my sense of direction, he's better off without me.*

Ethel looked at us. "He'll be alright." I wasn't sure if she was trying to convince herself or us, so I plastered a smile on my face and nodded.

"He'll be alright." I hated making that empty promise, but what else could I do besides glare at the back of Mahmud's head? No one else was speaking up, and Ethel had agreed with Julia. Mahmud had done what he had been threatening to do since the start of the trip and left someone behind. Humphry was on his own.

THE BUS PULLED into a gravelled yard decorated with colourful, flowering bushes.

"Ok everyone, this is where we are having lunch. It is the only kibbutz in Jerusalem and they grow all of their own food. We have to be at the Museum by 2 PM so please be back at bus in 45 minutes. Exactly 45 minutes. We don't want another Humphry."

"Come on Ethel," Emily put her arm around the older woman's shoulders. "Come sit at our table for lunch."

I followed them into the very clean and air-conditioned self-service cafeteria. In the middle of the room were various tables piled high with delicious looking food. One table was dedicated just for salads. Eggplant salad, lentil salad, bean salad, and every other salad imaginable. Everything was delicious and tasted incredibly fresh. The best part was, it was half the price of the horrid lunch Mahmud had ambushed us with yesterday.

For the first time since the start of the tour, everyone was waiting in front of the bus before the designated leave time. Our memory of Humphry's fate was very fresh in our minds.

Julia looked around the courtyard and frowned. "Has anyone seen Mahmud? No? Well, I'm sure he'll be here soon."

We waited outside in the sun for 10 minutes before he turned up, grinning and unapologetic. Julia smacked him on the arm with her clipboard and spoke sharply in Hebrew, wiping the smile off his face. I grinned and climbed onto the bus feeling a little happier. After leaving poor Humphry behind like that, I had very little sympathy for Mahmud and seeing Julia smack him had been the high-light of my day.

"Good news," Emily whispered in my ear. "Humphry is back at the hotel."

"How do you know?" I asked without looking away from the Dead Sea Scrolls on display.

"I heard Julia tell Ethel that he checked into the hotel. Thank goodness!"

I nodded, my eyes firmly fixed on the scroll fragments behind the thick glass. "I was worried he would get lost trying to get back to the hotel."

"What are you doing? Are you trying to *read* the scrolls?"

"Oh sorry," I looked at Emily and grinned. "Not quite. I was trying to pick out the letters of the alphabet that I know."

Emily raised her eyebrows. "Since when can you read ancient Hebrew?"

"Can't. But lucky for me, a lot of it is written in the same style of modern Hebrew so I can recognise some letters." I turned back to the display. "Did I ever tell you that I wanted to be an archaeologist when I was younger?"

"What do you mean younger? You are young!"

I rolled my eyes. "I mean, as a kid. I wanted to be an archaeologist like Indiana Jones. My favourite school excursion of all time was the visit to the ancient Egyptian exhibit in the Turin museum."

"So why didn't you?"

"I chose anthropology instead, but I still love ancient history."

"Well, don't get too distracted trying to translate these ancient scrolls or Mahmud will leave you behind Humphry. I'm heading back to the bus."

I nodded and stopped playing my little game. There was still half the room to see and I didn't want to get left behind. Although, getting left at the museum might not be so bad...

"Time for the bus," Julia announced from the exit door.

Damn! I hurried around the room, trying to look at everything before running out with a couple of other stragglers. The bus engine was already running and Julia was standing with one foot on the stairs and the other on the ground.

"Thanks Julia!" I said breathlessly and hopped on.

"Where have you been?" Emily scolded. "I was about to get off the bus and come look for you! I didn't want you to be left here alone."

"Sorry, I just got so caught up, and time flew by!"

"That's ok. I was talking to Ethel about tonight's free time. What do you think about having ice-cream with them in the New City? We could hang out there tonight instead of the Old City."

"Sounds good. We haven't been to the New City at night, and I'd love to see the night vibe."

"Ok, great. I'll tell Ethel to meet us outside the hotel at 6?"

I nodded and leaned back in my chair. The day was definitely improving. Humphry had turned up safe at the hotel, I got to see the Dead Sea Scrolls, and now I had a relaxing evening and ice-cream with friends to look forward to.

"You all disappeared!" Humphry accused us as soon as we were within earshot. "I sat down for two minutes and you all disappeared."

"Peter went to look for you but *you* had disappeared," Emily joked back.

Ethel looked at us and sighed. "He probably fell asleep somewhere."

"Hahaha," I chuckled weakly, my conscience uneasy. "Sorry Humphry."

"No harm done, I made it back alright."

Luckily, I thought grimly. It could have been so much worse but there was no point dwelling on what if scenarios. "How about some ice-cream to cheer us all up?"

"Lead on, you two are our Jerusalem tour guides again," Humphry said.

I wasn't as familiar with the New City as the Old City, but I knew where to find good ice-cream and how to order it in Hebrew so I volunteered for the job. I walked into the crowded ice cream shop and waited for my turn. And waited.

Wait a minute! Didn't those people come after me? I'm sure they did...

New people walked into the shop, walked right up to the already crowded counter and started yelling their order like everyone else seemed to be doing.

I turned to look at the older man standing next to me. His white beard and moustache, and round figure reminded me strongly of Santa Clause. "Excuse me, is this the line?"

He laughed and nodded, then stepped up and yelled something in Hebrew at the staff. One of the girls looked at him and nodded.

"Go," he nudged his head towards the ice-cream girl behind the counter. "Or you will never get your turn."

"But you were here before me," I protested.

"Is ok, go," he said with a kind smile.

"Toda Raba *(thank you very much!)*," I told him in Hebrew and walked up to the counter. It was so crowded I couldn't actually see the ice-cream so I stood on my tip toes and yelled out my order in Hebrew. I only knew a few flavours so my travel companions would have to be satisfied with what I got. Luckily for me, the ice-cream was delicious and no one complained.

Dinner in the New City was a different experience to the Old City. There were so many options; cafés, restaurants, take away stores with a Jerusalem twist like a take-away bagel shop, or the more internationally recognised ones like McDonald's. Humphry wanted a hamburger so we went into the empty McDonald's. The teenage girl at the register was very busy flirting with *two* teenage boys who were supposed to be cooking.

"Shalom," I said in Hebrew but was ignored completely.

One of the boys was playing with the girl's hair, while the other boy leaned on the counter and flexed his muscles.

"Excuse me," Emily tried with no success.

"Maybe we should go somewhere else," Ethel suggested.

"No," Humphry said obstinately. "I want my burger."

"I don't think they care," I muttered to Emily and laughed.

Apparently teenagers were the same wherever you went in the world.

We waited for a few more minutes, Ethel trying to keep Humphry from making a scene.

Eventually, one of the boys thrust his head towards us. "What you want?"

"I want a hamburger with fries and coke," Humphry told him, his tone half amused and half annoyed. "With pickles."

The girl sighed and tapped the order onto the computer screen. The boys, very reluctantly, headed towards the kitchen area to cook Humphry's hamburger and resumed their flirting as soon as it was served.

"You girls sure you don't want hamburgers?" Humphry asked between bites.

"We're having bagels," Emily told him.

"Just bagels?" Ethel asked.

"With a Jerusalem twist. It's a takeaway shop, and you order whatever filling you like in your bagel," I clarified. "I'm having smoked salmon and cream cheese."

"I'm having one with a vegetable filling," Emily told them.

"Sounds lovely dear," said Ethel, delicately munching on a chip.

I grinned. Besides the sightseeing and souvenir shopping, my favourite thing about Israel so far was the incredibly fresh food. Good thing I was walking so much every day, or I would have to buy looser clothes.

CHAPTER 11
KIBBUTZ

There is so much to see in Israel so on our way to the Golan Heights, we made several sightseeing stops. The first one was Qasr el Yahud, Jesus's baptism site along the Jordan River. In the middle of a desert like place, two young bored soldiers guarded the crumbling buildings near the river. The water was a murky green, and despite the reputed miraculous healing properties, I was not tempted to touch it. Between the alarming shade of water colour and signs warning of mines, I was not sorry when Julia herded us back onto the bus. Our next destination was Beit She'an (also known as Beth Shean), an exquisitely preserved town of Roman-Byzantine ruins. We had less than an hour to explore and take photos before getting back on the bus. The next stop was Nazareth.

"Pay attention everyone," Julia called out from the front of the bus. "See that wall behind me? The Church of the Annunciation is in there."

"Does she mean the wall behind the giant sign that says 'Islam is the only one and true religion'?" I whispered to Emily.

"I guess so," she whispered back and leaned forward to hear Julia.

"Now, this is very interesting Church. Every Catholic community from around world sent a mosaic of Mary and baby Jesus," Julia explained. "Enjoy looking at them and taking pictures, but we leave in 30 minutes so please be back at the bus in time. We walk from here."

I followed the others down the road to the Church, which was surrounded by a large, thick, stone wall that formed a closed courtyard around the building.

"You can take pictures here and inside Church," Julia told our group. "Have fun."

Eyes wide, I turned 360 degrees on the spot. Everywhere I looked were the most exquisite mosaics displayed on the courtyard walls. Camera in hand, I walked around slowly. Of all the Churches we had seen so far, this was definitely my favourite! I was fascinated with how Mary and Jesus were depicted by each nation, interpreted and represented differently through national and cultural influences. The Irish mosaic had a very Celtic looking Mary, and the Japanese mosaic depicted Mary wearing a lovely kimono with beautiful almond shaped eyes. The Spanish Mary had dark hair and the Italian Mary was blonde, but in every mosaic she always had a look of kindness on her face.

Before I knew it, it was time to leave. Lunch was a quick stop at a gas station with two options for food, a falafel wrap or a shawarma wrap, neither of which looked particularly appetizing. Back on the bus to Safed, the centre of Kabbalah and Jewish mysticism.

Julia led the way through the narrow streets and alleys, up and down steep stairways, through the Artists' Quarter and Synagogue Quarter. It was rushed. We had a few minutes inside one of the synagogues and then followed Julia back to the bus. Well, until we lost sight of her when she turned down a lane with half of the group and disappeared into thin air.

"Which way did she turn? Left or right?" Tiffany demanded.

"I don't know! I was taking a photo," Peter answered.

"We should wait here. Julia will come back for us," Emily suggested.

"Oh yea? And what if Mahmud decides to leave without us?" Asked Jean.

"They wouldn't," Peter told her. "Half of the group is here. They'll have to come look for us"

"We'll send out scouts to look for Julia and the others. They either went left or right. We'll just go down those lanes and see if we can find them, then come back," Peter's Uncle Jack said.

"No, we should stick together or we will get even more lost," Valeria argued.

"We won't go far, just down the lanes to see if we can spot the rest of the group. Come on Uncle Jack, I'll go down the left lane."

The rest of us waited for our scouts to return, and with each minute they were gone, the group's anxiety rose. Their return, even though the mission was unsuccessful, was celebrated but nothing like the cheers that erupted when we spotted Julia's cowboy hat almost 20 minutes later. This time, we followed her closely like little ducklings until we were all safely on the bus. Mahmud didn't waste any time in turning the engine on and starting to turn the enormous vehicle.

Julia tapped on the microphone to get our attention. "Now that we are all back together, we can finally leave. For the next two nights, we are staying in a kibbutz in the Golan Heights. For those who don't know, kibbutz is a community of people who share the work and grow their own food. It is like a big family and this one is near the Lebanese border. It is a very pretty area, and we will stop for some photos along the way. Ok Mahmud, let's go."

Mahmud grumbled something in Hebrew which made Julia frown. A large tourist bus had just pulled up behind ours, making it impossible for Mahmud to drive past it.

"One of the buses will have to reverse," Humphrey pointed out the obvious.

"My money is on Mahmud," I joked to Emily. "He won't reverse."

Emily laughed. "Probably."

"Oooh, it's like a Mexican stand-off," Jean giggled.

Mahmud was convinced he had right of way and gestured to the other driver to reverse.

The other driver shook his head.

Mahmud frowned, rolled up his sleeves and got off the bus.

"They're going to fight!" Someone yelled out and the passengers across the aisle clambered over to our side to stare out the windows.

Short, stocky, grumpy Mahmud marched up to the other bus, waving his arms and shouting. The other driver hesitated for a moment, then slowly, ever so slowly, began reversing his bus.

"Yaaaaaay!"

"Woooooo!"

"Go Mahmud!"

"You showed him!"

Mahmud climbed onto the bus grinning and savouring his hero's welcome.

"Okay, enough excitement for today," Julia ordered. "Let's go to the kibbutz!"

THE DRIVE through the Golan Heights was relaxing and we arrived at the picturesque kibbutz in the late afternoon. Set among trees and flowering shrubs, with an outdoor pool, an indoor sauna and lovely gardens, it looked like a health resort. Our room was simply furnished but clean and comfortable. We had the whole afternoon free so after a long walk around the kibbutz and getting sunburnt, we lounged by the swimming pool until dinner time.

Like the kibbutz in Jerusalem, the meal area was set up to be self-serve. The impressive choice of food was displayed on the left, while tables and chairs took up the rest of the room. I piled my plate as high as politely permissible, devoured it and went back for more. Of all the delicious meals I had eaten in Israel, this was by far the best. The vegetables were perfectly roasted; the meat melted on my tongue, the salad was crisp and refreshing.

I couldn't believe how good everything tasted. How could a simple tomato be so delicious? I had never tasted anything so fresh or full of flavour.

"Why do you look so glum?" Emily asked, her plate full of vegetables and a variety of salads. "Don't you like the food?"

"That's the problem. This meal has ruined all the future meals I will have. Nothing will taste as good as this, and now I'll be comparing everything to this standard!"

Laughing, Emily reached for a bread roll from the basket. "Save room for dessert."

BREAKFAST the next morning was just as incredible. Everything was grown and prepared at the kibbutz, including the creamy yogurt and golden honey. It was a feast and the perfect way to start the day.

The morning's itinerary focused on visiting the ancient ruins of Capernaum and a boat ride on the Sea of Galilee, which turned out to be a large freshwater lake, in a quaint wooden boat. With calm waters, a cooling breeze and the sound of birds chirping above, it was a very calming and relaxing experience. Until the ship's captain put on a CD of dramatic music. He opened a small box full of trinkets and stood next to it, staring at the group with an expectant expression. All the way back to shore. Not that it made a difference, no one bought anything.

· · ·

"I CAN'T BELIEVE how hungry I am," I told Emily. "I had a big breakfast and have hardly walked all morning!"

"I'm hungry too," she admitted. "I hope we stop somewhere nice for lunch."

"Ahem," Julia coughed into her microphone. "We're having lunch at a special restaurant today. They serve Saint Peters Fish, which is famous for the story in the Bible where Jesus told his disciple to pull out a fish from the Sea of Galilee and use the gold coin in its mouth to pay taxes. Now, the restaurant catches the fish fresh every day and grilles it whole. It is very delicious but it is an optional lunch so it is not included in the price of your tour. If you want to eat in restaurant, it is 80 shekels per person."

"80 shekels per person for grilled fish?" I muttered to Emily.

"Hang on, when you say the whole fish – do you mean the head is still there?" Tiffany asked loudly.

"Of course," Julia answered. "Maybe you also will find the gold coin in its mouth."

Laughter rippled through the group.

"What if we don't like fish?" Humphrey asked. "Is there somewhere close by we can eat?"

Julia turned to speak to Mahmud in Hebrew.

"How many people want to eat Saint Peter's Fish?" She asked the group.

Less than five people raised their hands.

"Hmmm. How many of you *don't* want to eat the fish?" She asked.

Most of the group raised their hands, including me and Emily.

"Okay, I will talk with Mahmud and see if we can go somewhere else. But since we are here already, those that want to eat fish come into the restaurant with me and Mahmud. I will try to find somewhere else to eat for the others and come out and tell you. There is a beach and you can relax there for a little while."

"I hope she doesn't take long to find somewhere else. Can you hear my stomach grumbling?" I asked Emily.

She laughed and hopped off the bus. "Lucky for you there is a kiosk on this beach," she pointed to a small hut near the shore. "We can have some ice cream while we wait."

Valeria and her children, Tiffany and Jean, Humphry and Ethel and a few others had already lined up to buy ice cream. By the time it was my turn they were sold out and my only option was a slice of pizza which the young attendant tried to sell for 17 shekels, per slice.

"Can you warm up the pizza?" I asked him.

"No microwave."

I hesitated, looking at the mostly empty takeaway pizza box next to him.

A kiosk with only 1 pizza box and no microwave? Maybe it was his lunch? I'll pass.

Disappointed and hungry, I joined Emily, Tiffany, Jean and Valeria cooling their bare feet in the water, waiting for Julia and Mahmud to take us somewhere else for lunch.

Almost an hour later, when our skirts and dresses had been repeatedly splashed by the waves, Julia, Mahmud and the few tour members who had opted for St Peter's Fish emerged from the restaurant.

Mahmud took one look at Tiffany's wet sun dress and started yelling and waving his arms. Julia put up her hands to calm him, but he kept shaking his head and yelling.

Sighing, Julia walked up to Tiffany and very politely explained that Mahmud was worried she would get his bus seat wet, and asked her to wrap a towel around her waist.

I leaned closer to Emily said quietly, "Our skirts and Valeria's dress are also wet. Why isn't she asking us to wrap a towel around too?"

"Our skirts haven't gone see through in the water."

"Ah, I see… "

While Mahmud and Tiffany argued, I seized the opportunity and snuck onto the bus before I got into trouble for having a wet skirt. It wasn't that wet, but I didn't want to risk being yelled at in front of everyone.

Julia managed to secure a truce between Mahmud and Tiffany. After counting our heads, and double checking that Humphry was on the bus, she nodded to Mahmud and he started the engine.

"Where are we going for lunch?" Peter asked what everyone else wanted to know.

"Ah, I am sorry. We don't have time to stop anywhere else now. We have to be at the diamond factory soon before they close."

"What? I haven't had any lunch at all!"

"This is ridiculous!"

"What about those of us who haven't eaten?"

"There was kiosk on beach. Why you not buy from there?" Julia asked.

"All they had was ice cream and cold pizza," Valeria told her.

Julia shook her head, her lips pressed tight. "I am sorry. We are on tight schedule and have to go to diamond factory. But, you will have a good dinner tonight at the Kibbutz."

That was not the answer we wanted to hear and people grumbled for a good five minutes after the announcement. I sulked in my seat, hungry and annoyed that I had run out of snacks. With little free time and no access to local markets, I hadn't been able to stock up on snacks and water bottles since Jerusalem.

I miss Jerusalem, I thought glumly. *As interesting as everything is on the tour, nothing beats the colourful chaos of the Old City.*

Sighing, I pushed my reclining chair back and day-dreamed of Jerusalem all the way to the diamond factory. This was one stop on the itinerary I would have happily skipped. I wasn't interested in diamonds and there was no chance that I could afford to buy one as a gift for mum. I couldn't wait to get back to the kibbutz and have a delicious dinner.

"You know, until I came to Israel I had no idea there were so many salads," I told Emily, generously piling my plate.

"Vegan heaven." She smiled and picked up her cutlery. "Have you noticed that the food tonight is all cold?"

"Cold?"

"As in, not cooked. Everything is fresh or pre-cooked like boiled eggs," she pointed out.

"Oh yeah, you're right. I didn't even realise until you mentioned it. Wow, is it the Sabbath already? The week has flown by!"

Emily nudged her head towards a free table. "I'll save a spot for you."

"Ok, I'll just get some water."

Carefully balancing my full glass, cutlery and plate of salads, I walked through the tables and sat across from Emily.

"I love this chickpea salad," Emily said. "I hope the food will be as nice in Jordan."

"Me too, but I intend to make the most of it while we're in Israel."

"Shame that tomorrow is the last day." Emily sipped her water.

"Yea, I really like this kibbutz. I wish we could stay longer."

"I wish we could stay longer in Israel."

I raised my eyebrows, my mouth too busy chewing to ask what she meant.

Emily laughed. "You've completely lost track of time. Tomorrow is our last day in Israel. We're off to Jordan after that."

My fork paused in mid-air. "No! Are you sure?"

"Yes. Haven't you been reading the itinerary?"

I shook my head and reached for my water just as an

empty wine glass appeared next to it. My head turned to the waiter in the crisp white shirt and black pants. He placed an empty wine glass in front of Emily and began filling it up.

Emily looked at me and mouthed, "Did you order this?"

Eyes wide, I shook my head.

"Excuse me," I looked up at the waiter. "We didn't order wine."

Smiling, he began filling my glass. "It iz with complimentz from the manager."

I glanced at Emily who looked stunned. "Um, but... we don't know the manager."

The waiter grinned and indicated with his head to a man across the room. "That guy with ze white shirt."

I twisted in my seat to see. The man looked up from the plate he was holding, caught me staring and nodded, a smile playing on his lips.

Blushing furiously, I looked at Emily who was sitting very still, eyes wide and a deep red colouring her cheeks.

Oh my gosh, this is like the movies! This has never happened to me in Australia. What do I do? Is it rude to refuse? He's already poured the wine. I don't even like wine. Don't make a fool of yourself, be calm and poised like a sophisticated woman.

"Um, thank you but I don't drink," I half whispered to the waiter.

His dark eyes stared boldly at my face. "Iz ok, have a little. Manager's name is Oren. You enjoy, he chat to you later." With a cheeky grin, he sauntered off.

I turned to Emily who was giggling. "My friend Erica was right. The men in Israel are gallant. This never happened to me in Australia," she said.

Glancing over my shoulder to make sure the manager wasn't looking, I discreetly emptied my glass into the pot plant next to the table while Emily smothered a laugh behind her hand.

"Hurry, Humphry's coming over," she said, still laughing.

"You girls coming to the bar? Me and the missus are

having a drink after dinner to celebrate the tour. Julia and the others will be there too."

"I can't believe it's almost over," I said to no one in particular.

"Sounds good, we'll meet you there," Emily told him.

By the time we had finished our meal and walked over to the bar which opened up into the garden, the rest of the group was there.

"Over here girls," Ethel called out, waving her arm. "We saved you a seat."

Peter and his uncle Jack, Valeria and her children Sophie and Mark, and Julia were already sitting down. The rest of the group was scattered at other tables or in the garden.

"So, have you enjoyed the tour of Israel?" Julia asked.

"Oh, yes!" Ethel said.

Valeria nodded, her dark fringe bouncing. "Very good."

"It's been incredible," Peter told her and his uncle Jack nodded in agreement.

"I don't really want to leave," Emily said.

"It's been great." Humphry drained his glass of beer. "Who's continuing to Egypt?"

"We are," Peter said.

"Wait," I frowned. "What are you talking about? The tour is going to Jordan."

"Oh no, dear," Ethel contradicted. "We are going to Egypt."

"But… but we booked a tour for Israel and Jordan."

"That's right, we did," Emily backed me up.

Julia glanced from me to Emily. "Didn't your travel agent tell you? This tour group was only for Israel. After that, it breaks up and people go to other places. You two are going to Jordan and others are going to Egypt."

"We thought the tour went to both countries," Emily said.

"I am sorry," Julia shook her head. "My company only does tours of Israel. The other tours for Jordan, Turkey and Egypt are subcontracted to local companies."

My mouth opened and closed like a fish, but no sound came out.

"Oh dear!" Ethel clutched her glass. "Oh, how sad – you won't be going to Egypt with us."

"Let me see your travel documents," Julia put out her hand.

Digging into her handbag, Emily pulled out the documents and handed them over.

"Ah, I see. Your itinerary says border transfer to Jordan."

"What does that mean?" I asked Julia. "I assumed it meant our tour bus will drive across the border into Jordan."

"Other people in the group are going to Jordan, but they are flying from Tel Aviv to Amman. Your documents say border transfer, so you will have to cross the border by land," Julia explained.

"What?!" Emily yelped. "On our own?"

"The company will have organised for someone to pick you up from the border in Jordan but I don't know how you will get there. Are you sure your travel agent didn't say anything?"

"Absolutely nothing," Emily said, a hint of annoyance in her voice.

"I will call my head office and find out how you will get to the border," Julia offered. "But it is the Sabbath now and everything is closed until tomorrow sunset. Don't worry girls, I will help you to get to the border. Maybe we have to book a taxi. For now, just enjoy your time in Israel."

"Thank you for helping," Emily said.

Julia nodded and stood. "I will go check on the others. The Kibbutz is having a party for the children who live here. They have a clown who does magic outside in garden. You should go watch, enjoy the night and don't stress."

No chance of that. My stress levels had already shot through the roof.

"Not to worry, girls," Humphry said with a grin. "I have

the perfect solution. You two are pretty small so I will smuggle you into Egypt in my suitcase."

I burst out laughing. "If we can't sort out our transfer, I'm going back to the Old City."

"Take your mind off it for tonight," Peter advised. "How often do you get to enjoy a party at a kibbutz?"

"You're right," Emily told him. "We might as well enjoy tonight."

I followed them outside but I wasn't in a party mood. Loud music blared from the speakers and the clown was performing his magic tricks to a few half interested adults. Children ran around popping soap bubbles, while their parents sat under the starry sky, chatting and enjoying life. The bonds of community were strong, and they extended the hospitality to us.

The stars were bright, the scent of flowers lingered in the air and the cool breeze was delightful. My shoulders loosened. Life on the kibbutz seemed quite wonderful.

CHAPTER 12
BAGELS ON THE BEACH

The day had passed in a frenzy of hopping on and off the bus, posing for photos at various landmarks and long hours of driving. We were driving down the coast of Israel and although the scenery was spectacular, I had only one thing on my mind – the border transfer. It was already in the afternoon and we were headed to the hotel in Tel Aviv, and we still didn't know what would happen tomorrow. My anxiety levels were increasing every hour.

The tour was over, and everyone would be dropped off at the different hotels. Emily and I had been booked into the same hotel we stayed at in our first time in Tel Aviv, along with Valeria and her children, Sophie and Mark. Humphrey and Ethel were staying in a hotel close by and we had already organised to all have dinner together on the beach.

I rubbed my neck with one hand, trying to ease the tension, while I flicked through the photos on my camera. The charming old town of Acre (also known as Akko) brought a smile to my face. It was the most complete and well preserved old town in Israel and dated back to the Hellenistic period. I much preferred the old cities with character and history to modern cities full of skyscrapers. My thumb pushed down on the camera button, flicking through my photos of the city of Haifa and its beautiful Baha'i Shrine and gardens, the Crusader fortress in Caesarea and the old town of Jaffa. I loved the artists' quarter in Jaffa; it was like an open air art exhibit.

Emily gently nudged my elbow. "I'll check my email as soon as we get to the hotel. Hopefully our travel agent has responded."

Nodding, I slipped my camera back into my backpack. "I'm going to try and call the Jordanian head office. They might know something."

"Julia said she would get in touch with the Israeli head office after sundown."

"I doubt they would open on a Saturday evening. Anyway, it won't hurt to try. Julia gave me the number for the Israeli head office and the Jordanian one, so I'll call both. Let's hope that somebody picks up and can tell us what is going on."

Julia walked down the middle of the bus towards us. "Your hotel is first drop off. I will take others to hotels, but after I will call my boss and find out about your transfer. I'll leave a message for you at the hotel reception."

"Thank you so much," Emily said with a smile.

Julia nodded once and walked back to the front of the bus to oversee the drop-off. I grabbed my backpack and put it on my lap, ready for the signal from the front. We had already said our goodbyes earlier, as instructed, and were poised at the edge of our seats ready to get off as quickly as possible. The whole thing was rushed and unnecessarily stressful.

"I'M glad we're back at the same hotel." Emily said.

"Mmm," I mumbled distractedly. "I'm going to the lobby to make those phone calls."

"Don't you want to unpack first?"

"I'll do it later."

"Okay, I'll check my email." Emily said and headed straight for the computers.

I nodded and walked to the hotel reception, dragging my suitcase behind me. I tried the Jordanian office first but no one picked up the phone. I called the Israeli office, but as I had expected, no one answered. I called the Jordanian office again. No answer.

"Any luck?" she asked.

I turned around and shook my head. "It just rings through and there is not even an answering machine. What about you? Did the travel agent respond to our email?"

"Yes, but it was completely useless."

I groaned. "What did she say?"

"Pretty much what we have already done – talk to our tour guide. Oh, and she wished us a good trip."

"Great," my voice dripped with sarcasm. "So no help from there, Julia doesn't know what's happening, and I can't get in touch with the head office."

"Don't stress, we'll sort this out."

I shot her an irritated look. "You seem to be taking this very calmly."

Emily shrugged. "If we can't sort it out, I'd be happy to stay in Tel Aviv for the next few days until our flight leaves."

"You're forgetting that our flight is booked to leave from Jordan."

"Come on, let's go unpack and walk down to the beach."

"Fine," I grumbled. "But let me call one more time. Just in case someone answers."

My fingers dialled the number automatically.

Ring, ring, ring, ring…

Sighing, I moved to put the receiver down and froze.

"Ello? Elooo?"

Am I hearing things?

"Hello?" *Please don't let me be hallucinating!*

•

175

"Yes?" A man answered.

Clutching the phone, I twisted to look at Emily and motioned for her to move closer so she could hear the conversation. The good news was that the Jordanian tour director was expecting us and had organised for someone to pick us up from their side of the border. The bad news was that the Israeli office was supposed to organise the transfer to the Israeli side of the border.

I looked at Emily with raised eyebrows. "Well, at least now we know who was responsible for organising our transfer, but we can't get in touch with them."

"Julia might have more luck. Let's go pack our suitcases so we can meet the others for dinner. We'll try calling the Israeli office after sundown."

"Alright, just give me a minute to send an email. I promised my family I would keep them updated."

TRYING to fit all the gifts I had bought into my suitcase temporarily took my mind off the border problem. Still, I couldn't relax and enjoy my last evening in Israel. Before leaving the hotel, I stopped at the reception desk and checked if Julia had left any messages for us. No luck. There was no point calling the Israeli office because the Sabbath hadn't finished. Resigned, I went outside to meet Emily and the others.

"Any luck?" Humphrey asked.

I shook my head glumly. "Where's Ethel?"

"Resting. She's not feeling very well. It's very hot here for her."

"What a shame," Valeria said. "I hope she feels better soon."

Humphrey nodded thanks. "I won't be joining you for dinner, but I wanted to say goodbye and wish you luck. If you change your mind, I'll smuggle you to Egypt in my suitcases."

I laughed. "I believe you. Thank you for coming to say goodbye, and please tell Ethel goodbye for us."

"Enjoy your Egyptian adventure," Emily told him.

Waving, Humphrey turned and walked back to his hotel down the road.

"It's just the five of us then," Valeria said. "Do you still want to go to the beach?"

Her children, Mark and Sophie, nodded quickly. They were the quietest, and politest, pair of teenagers I have ever seen.

"Yes," Emily answered. "I hope they have something to eat nearby because I'm hungry."

Laughter and loud music floated from the beach. Smiling, I stepped onto the soft, warm sand and for the first time all day, my shoulders loosened. It was as crowded as the last time I had been here. Old ladies sitting on beach chairs, waist deep in the water, young people playing ping pong, children running around screeching with excitement.

"Ooo, look at that bagel," I stared shamelessly as the man walked past. "Where did he get it from?"

"Over there," Valeria pointed to a small building that looked halfway between a beach hut and a shop. "You can order the bagels stuffed with what you like, and they can grill it for you."

"I vote bagels for dinner," Emily raised her hand.

"Yes!" Mark said with a little jump. "Me too, I want bagels for dinner too."

His older sister nodded her head, flicking her perfectly straight, long, blond hair behind her shoulder. "I like bagels too."

Valeria looked at me and I grinned. "I love bagels."

"We all want them," she smiled. "Tell me what you want and I can go order them. Someone needs to stay here and save our spot on the beach."

"I'll help you carry them back," I offered.

"Vegan for me," Emily reminded me.

Our spot securely guarded by the two teenagers and Emily, Valeria and I walked over to the very busy bagel hut. Three young men worked frantically behind the hot plate, stuffing and grilling bagels, while people crowded around the stall and shouted their orders.

"If we wait for our turn like in Europe, we'll be here all night," Valeria told me. "Tell me what you like and I will order it in Hebrew."

"You can speak Hebrew?"

"Of course, I am Jewish. I come to Israel many times."

"I wish I had known earlier! I could have practiced my Hebrew with you!"

Valeria smiled. "We'll practice after dinner." Leaning forward, she yelled out our orders and we stepped back to wait, while more people pushed to the front.

In his rush to complete several orders at the same time, the bagel boy making our order burned mine and put the wrong fillings in Valeria's, as well as in an Israeli woman's order.

Valeria requested him to re- make her order, with the correct ingredients.

He refused and shoved the burned bagel towards me.

Valeria shook her head and pushed it back to him, pointing at the charcoal burned outside.

I tried to ask in English if he could make me another one. It was inedible.

The Israeli woman complained loudly about her bagel.

Bagel boy frowned, started waving his arms around and yelling in Hebrew.

Valeria and the Israeli woman argued back.

The two other young men tried to talk to him, pointing to empty bagels and the toaster. I guessed they were telling him to remake the orders. Bagel boy shushed them with his hands, and continued to argue with us.

Hungry, I was about to admit defeat and eat my burned dinner when one of the other young men picked up fresh bagels and began re-making our orders.

"What took you so long?" Mark asked his mother.

"The best customer service I've ever had," she said.

Laughing, I told them what happened. The wait had been worth it. With the sun setting in the background and the happy atmosphere, I bet even the burned bagel would have tasted good.

"GIVE ME A MINUTE," I told Emily. "I want to try calling the Israeli office one more time."

"We've been trying for half an hour and no one is answering. I'm more worried about not having heard back from Julia."

I dialled the number again, crossing my fingers but not getting my hopes up.

Ring, ring, ring.

"Ello, how can I help?"

I gasped. Worried that it was too good to be true, I asked if this was the National head office for the tour company. When the man confirmed, I almost started crying with relief. I explained our dilemma and gave him all the details of our booking and our tour guide's name.

"Tsk, tsk. But you no receive letter?"

"What letter?" I demanded.

"Ze one we send to travel agent in Australia. We send two letters. Australia and hotel lobby. No one give you letter?"

"No," I fumed. *That's the last time I book with that travel agency!*

"Is all arranged. Driver will pick you up in private car tomorrow morning at 8.30. He pick you up from hotel and take you to border."

"Thank you so much!"

"Not problem. Enjoy trip." Click. He hung up.

"Did you hear that?" I asked Emily who had her ear pressed to the other side of the receiver.

Nodding, she jumped up from the stool. "I'll ask the reception desk about this letter."

"Hang on, I'll come too."

"Excuse me," Emily asked an elegant looking young woman behind the desk. "Have you received any messages for us?" She handed over our room key and travel documents with our names printed on top.

The receptionist checked the computer and pigeon hole behind her. "No messages."

"Are you sure? We were told there should be a letter for us here at reception," I told her.

The young woman shrugged and turned to her colleague, speaking in rapid Hebrew. Her colleague had a look on the computer and checked the papers on the reception desk.

"No messages."

Sighing, I turned to Emily. "Never mind. At least now we know what to do."

"Thanks for checking," Emily told the young women as we turned to leave.

"Wait minute please," one of the young women said.

"Yes?" I asked eagerly. "Have you found something?"

She picked up an envelope with our names written on it and held it out. "This is you?"

"Yes, that's us," Emily confirmed.

I opened the envelope to find a scribbled note from Julia saying we would be picked up from the hotel and driven to the border tomorrow morning.

"Oh, she must have stopped by while we were at the beach," Emily said, reading over my shoulder.

"This would have been extremely useful to know before we spent $40 dollars calling the Jordanian and Israeli offices," I grumbled.

Between the travel agent not giving us our letter, the reception desk either not receiving it or losing it, I had spent my last day in Israel stressing about something that should have been taken care of before the trip had begun.

"It's done now," Emily said in an annoyingly calm voice. "Let's cheer up by looking at the souvenir shop in the lobby. It's still open and I still have some shekels to spend."

"Don't we have enough souvenirs?" I followed her into the shop anyway.

A thin old man towered over the counter.

"Shalom," he said with a smile, his blue eyes twinkling.

I smiled back. "Shalom." The little shop was full of wonderful things from jewellery to hand made good luck charms. I had no intention of buying anything, but somehow ended up spending all my shekels. Then I remembered we would need to tip the driver tomorrow morning.

"Excuse me, is there an ATM nearby? I need to withdraw cash."

He nodded, carefully placed our purchases in paper bags and adjusted his kippa. "It iz outside hotel. Iz dark now and no safe. I come with you."

"Oh, please don't trouble yourself," I told him hurriedly but he was already walking towards the door, key in hand. "I'm sure we will be fine."

Shaking his head, he motioned for us to exit the shop and locked it. "No safe. I come with you and show you way."

"Um … well, ok … I guess."

We followed him around the corner of the hotel.

"ATM in there," he pointed inside the well-lit area with several security cameras behind glass doors. "I wait here."

"Ok, thank you," Emily told him and walked inside.

Now that we were here, I was glad he had come along and was waiting for us. The boisterous looking group of youth hanging around outside made me a little nervous. I withdrew cash and shoved most of it in my bra, leaving a few notes for my wallet. If I was getting mugged, they weren't going to get much.

The old man walked us back to the hotel lobby, wished us good night and a safe journey before returning to his small shop.

"Wow, that was so nice of him!" Emily said.

I smiled. We were strangers to him, he owed us nothing and he knew we weren't Jewish and didn't speak Hebrew, but he still went out of his way to help us. "It seems that human kindness and decency still exist," I told her. It was a wonderful memory for my last night in Israel.

CHAPTER 13

INVISIBLE BORDERS

B *eep, beep, bee-*
"I'm up, I'm up," I grumbled and smacked the alarm clock.

Sighing, I rolled out of bed and stretched. My suitcase was packed and all I had to do was get dressed and have breakfast. The border transfer was organised so it should be a stress-free morning, but my heart insisted on thumping against my rib cage.

Chewing on my bottom lip, I got ready for the day.

Everything will be fine, I told myself. *The transfer was organised by the tour and I am leaving, not entering Israel. There shouldn't be any problems. I hope…*

"Are you okay?" Emily asked. "You've hardly had any breakfast, and you're not your usual chatterbox self."

"I'm fine." I said, ignoring my racing heart and sweaty palms. The truth was, I couldn't stop thinking about my entry into Israel.

What if they don't let me out of the country? What if they don't let me into Jordan because I've been to Israel? What if I get arrested?

"There you are!" Humphrey waved from the front of the hotel.

Valeria, looking glamorous as always, smiled and waved.

Emily grinned and hugged them. "What are you two doing here?"

"We came to say goodbye and wish you a good journey," Valeria said.

"The missus says goodbye and good luck. She's very tired but wanted me to see you off."

For the first time this morning, my smile wasn't forced. "Tell Ethel we will miss you two. Thank you for coming to see us off, it's so nice of you. You too Valeria. Thank you for all the laughs last night. It was the best bagels on the beach!"

"Try not to get arrested at the border," Humphrey joked while Valeria and Emily laughed.

"ha ha ha," I joined in weakly.

"That must be our driver." Emily pointed to the only car parked in front of the hotel that wasn't a taxi.

A stocky, muscular, bald man with very dark sunglasses got out of a plain white car.

"Transfer to Jordan?"

"Yes," Emily said.

"You are Emily and Noor?"

"Yes," Emily answered and I nodded.

"Papers."

His poker face expression never changed as he checked our paperwork and put our suitcases in the boot of the car.

"I am Avi, your driver. Get in."

Humphrey gave us one last hug. "Have fun girls, and stay safe."

"Safe travels." Valeria kissed us on each cheek.

"Thank you so much for coming to say goodbye!" Emily slid into the back seat gracefully.

Waving, I scrambled into the back of the car. "Have fun in Egypt!"

Avi pulled away from the curb and joined the traffic.

"Are you sure you're okay?" Emily whispered. "You look so tense."

I forced a smile. "I'm fine. Avi, how far is it to the border?"

"Two hours."

"Oh good, we'll get there by 10.30. Have you been a driver for long?" I didn't really care, but chatting about mundane things helped calm my nerves.

"Yes."

My eyes drifted to the dashboard. The little needle indicating the speed was increasing steadily. My stomach tightened. We were zooming through the streets of Tel Aviv, weaving through the traffic.

"Is it normally this busy?" I chattered.

"Yes."

Avi put on the indicator to switch lanes. As soon as there was a gap, he steered the car in the next lane, and the next, and the next.

My hands clutched the seat beneath me.

He sped up and switched lanes.

"Oh my God!" I squeaked.

"Is ok," Avi rumbled from the front.

His poker face never changed. Speeding up, he overtook the cars in the lane we had vacated, heading straight towards the oncoming truck.

I closed my eyes and pictured my family's faces.

"Is ok." Avi said in his flat tone.

My eyes cracked open.

No on-coming traffic. I sighed in relief. We were back in the correct lane and had surpassed all other cars.

Emily yawned. "I might get some sleep. Woke up a bit early today."

"Good idea," I mumbled and shut my eyes firmly.

If Avi pulled any more tricks like that, I didn't want to see it. Better to die in my sleep than see the traffic speeding towards me.

"WAKE UP."

I jolted awake and rubbed my eyes. "Are we there yet?"

"Close. I will not go through border with you. I leave you at checkpoint and you walk."

"Um, okay … "

Emily blinked and put her sunglasses. "Is it just me or is it hotter here?"

"No, I'm hot too."

Avi pulled into an empty car park surrounded by a wire fence topped with barbed wire. He got out of the car, pulled out our luggage and held out his hand for a tip.

Emily fumbled with her wallet and as soon as the money touched his palm, he climbed back into the car and drove off, covering us with a layer of white dust.

"What a social butterfly," Emily said sarcastically, making me laugh. "Want a photo in front of the sign?"

I turned to look at the metal sign 'Welcome to Jordan'. "Sure, why not?"

We took turns posing for a photo before focusing on the task at hand.

"Where is the check in office?" Emily looked around the empty car park with no signs.

"Let's ask them," I nudged my head towards the two Israeli soldiers with machine guns, who had been ignoring us since Avi had driven off.

Dragging our suitcases behind us, we walked up to the small gate they guarded.

"Excuse me, is this the border to cross into Jordan?" I asked nervously.

No matter how many times I had seen machine guns casually strapped to the backs of young men in Israel, it still made me nervous.

One of the soldier's eyes flicked towards us. "You have weapons in bags?"

"What?! No! Of course not!"

"Go," he waved his hand and stepped aside to let us through the small gate.

A little surprised, I hurried through and looked back. "Is that it? Are we in Jordan now?"

"Go building," he said and turned his back.

I looked at the large, square and very plain building that looked like a hybrid between a prison and train station.

"Where's the entrance to this building?" Emily asked.

"Maybe it's on the other side."

It took a few minutes of walking around the building before we found the entrance. There was hardly anyone inside, or signs where to go.

"Let's line up behind that family," Emily suggested. "We'll ask the person behind the glass."

"It looks like a bank desk."

"I don't see anywhere else to go."

"True. Ok, might as well."

The family in front of us had several young children, and the women were covered from head to toe in the loose, black abaya that some Muslim women wear. Whatever they were doing didn't take long and soon it was our turn.

"Hello, is this where we cross into Jordan?" I asked.

The woman behind the glass eyed me with a frown. "No. Here you pay border tax."

"Oh, okay. Sure."

"I didn't know we had to pay a border tax to leave the country," Emily whispered.

"Me either," I murmured, digging into my wallet for money. Thank goodness the nice old man had taken us to the ATM last night!

"Go through there," the woman pointed towards an open shop like the ones in airports.

"Let's follow that family," Emily suggested.

I nodded and followed her. They seemed to know where to go and what to do, which would be more helpful than the officers we had encountered so far.

"I think we need to go there." I pointed to a female soldier sitting behind thick glass, under the sign 'Passport Control.'

There was no one in line so Emily went up to the counter. "Excuse me, is this where we can cross into Jordan?"

"Passport," the officer snapped.

Emily slid her passport under the glass screen.

"Go through there," she pointed to a glass door at the back of the building. "Next."

I stepped up and handed over my passport. Emily stood just behind me with the suitcases.

The officer flicked through my passport, frowning and shaking her head.

I swallowed hard.

Not again! Please, not again!

"You travelling together?" she pointed to Emily who was watching us.

"Yes."

"Why your passport no stamped?"

"Stamped? I don't know. They gave me a loose leaf visa."

She muttered something in Hebrew then switched back to English. "Why no stamp? Huh? Why no stamp?" she threw her hands up in the air.

My knees trembled.

"How you enter Israel with no stamp?"

"I don't know. I gave them my passport at the airport and this is how I got it back."

"Lazy, do no job well," she grumbled. "I stamp now."

Without looking up, she slid my passport back and flicked her hand in the direction of the door. I snatched it up and grabbed my suitcase.

"Quick, let's go," I hissed to Emily. "Before she changes her mind!"

Emily pushed the glass door open.

"Ouch! My eyes!" I squinted and slipped on my sunglasses quickly. "How can it be so bright?" I complained.

"Geez, they really need to put up some more signs," Emily said.

My eyes shielded from the sun's glare, I looked around. In

front of us was a small gate, and across the narrow street was a large bus shelter with benches.

"Where's our tour guide?"

"Maybe he's running late," Emily suggested.

"Might as well get comfortable then." I sat on the bench against the wall.

We waited, and waited.

Emily looked at her watch. "He's almost an hour late."

A middle aged Israeli soldier walked out of the building and sat next to us on the bench. "What you doing?"

"We're waiting for our tour guide to pick us up," Emily explained. "Someone is supposed to pick us up from the Jordanian border."

The soldier smiled. "You wait there," he pointed to the bus shelter across the street.

"Sorry, we'll go now." I grabbed my suitcase and headed to the bus shelter.

The family we had seen inside the building was sitting on the benches, and besides us, there was no one else around.

"I can't believe we're in Jordan!"

"I know!" Emily said. "I'm really looking forward to seeing Petra."

"How much longer is our tour guide going to be?"

Emily shrugged and drank the last of her water. "What exactly did the Jordanian tour guy tell you over the phone?"

"That someone was going to pick us up from the Jordanian border and take us to the hotel. He'll have our names on a piece of paper."

"Okay, I guess we'll just have to wait here until he turns up."

I pulled out my camera and scrolled through my photos of Israel to pass the time. Every now and then small groups of people came out of the building and walked across the street to the bus shelter, but Emily and I were the only Westerners.

Emily stood and stretched. "I'm going to get some more water."

"Where from?"

"I saw someone fill up their water bottle from a drinking fountain just over there." She pointed to the other side of the bus shelter. "Call me if our tour guide appears."

I chuckled. "Don't worry, I won't leave without you."

Emily walked away just as a bus pulled up in front of me and the afternoon's tranquillity changed in the blink of an eye. The people around me rushed to put their suitcases in the storage compartment under the bus and lined up at the door to have their passports checked by the two Israeli officers who had appeared out of nowhere. Their blue military style uniforms were confusing. Were they soldiers? Security guards? Border patrol?

Sitting contently in the shade, I sipped my water and watched them rush onto the bus.

I wonder where they are going?

The female officer, a stocky brunette with a powerful voice, smartly rounded people up and ushered them onto the bus. Her colleague, a handsome young man who looked like Prince Charming from a Disney movie, walked up to me with a smile.

Blushing, I patted down my hair and hoped it wasn't frizzy from the humidity.

"Are you catching the bus?" he asked.

"Oh, um, well... I'm waiting… "

He raised his perfect eyebrows.

"I mean, I'm waiting for my friend. And we're waiting for our tour guide to pick us up," I babbled, pointing to Emily who was splashing her face with water.

He smiled and walked back to the building across the street.

His colleague spotted me still sitting on the bench and shouted, "Are you getting bus?"

"Oh, no thanks. I'm waiting for our tour guide."

She shrugged, signalled to the bus driver to close the

doors and drive off and walked across the street to the building.

I looked over to wave to Emily but she was already walking back towards me, watching the bus pull away from the curb.

"What was that about?" Emily asked, holding a full water bottle.

I shrugged. "They kept asking me if I was catching the bus."

"What for? Where does the bus go?"

"No idea. I wish we had a phone so we could call the tour office. This is getting ridiculous; we've been waiting for hours!"

Emily was frowning. "Did that tour director say anything to you about catching a bus?"

"No. You don't think we should have caught that bus, do you? I mean, we don't even know where it goes … "

"I'm just wondering why they kept asking you if we were catching the bus."

"Yeah… " My stomach tightened into a knot.

What if that was the only bus for today? There's no taxis here. What will we do if our tour guide doesn't turn up?

I looked around the giant, empty bus terminal. A breeze drifted past, lifting the limp flag on the pole across the street.

That's funny, I wouldn't have thought that the Jordanian government would allow Israel to fly their flag in Jordan. Wait a minute! An Israeli flag! In Jordan?! Unless… ?

My head snapped towards Emily who was staring at the flag with her mouth hanging open.

"Is it possible the Jordanian government would allow Israel to fly their flag on their land as a diplomatic gesture?"

Emily lowered the hand covering her mouth and turned to look at me. "Maybe? Are you thinking what I'm thinking?"

"But – but, I mean, passport control, and checkpoint outside, and pointing outside and bus -"

"I think we might still be in Israel," Emily said sheepishly.

My mouth dropped open. "Two hours!" I squeaked. "We've been waiting for over two hours thinking we were in Jordan!"

Emily started laughing. "No wonder our tour guide isn't here," she said, gasping for air.

"Stop laughing, it's not funny!"

"Oh yeah? Then why are you trying not to laugh?" She giggled and I burst out laughing.

It took several minutes for the amusement to settle down, but the embarrassment remained. More people joined us, including a group of middle aged American tourists who were as clueless as us about the process of the border crossing. Our only option was to wait for the next bus, hoping there was one scheduled, and ask the driver.

The next bus arrived and after confirming with the driver that we needed to catch it to cross into Jordan, we bought tickets (thank goodness I still had some shekels left), loaded our luggage and climbed on board. The driver waited until the bus was almost full before leaving. Besides the American group, Emily and I were the only Westerners. Everyone else seemed to be Jordanians returning home.

"We are here. Thank you, goodbye," the driver called out and opened the doors.

"What? Already?" Emily looked at her watch. "It's only been a few minutes!"

I looked out the window at a large, square concrete building that had been painted white. The entire journey seemed to be an incredibly short drive in a large car park. A thin man with close cropped peppery hair stood outside with an A4 piece of paper with our names printed on.

"Emily, look," I pointed out the window.

"We must be in Jordan now. Poor man, I hope he hasn't been waiting for us to turn up, out here in the sun for hours…"

I cringed and followed Emily out of the bus.

"Welcome! Welcome to Jordan!" He flashed his brilliantly

white teeth. "I am Omar your driver. I have been waiting and waiting and you no come. Did you lost?"

I blushed. "Um, yeah, something like that."

"Sorry we kept you waiting," Emily said. "So sorry!"

"Is ok. Come, I take suitcases and we check passports."

Omar marched up to the bus luggage storage and we pointed to our suitcases.

"I can't believe it. I can't believe we are in Jordan," I told Emily. "It takes me longer to get to my local gym than the time it took to cross the border from Israel to Jordan."

"I know. I thought it would be a much longer drive."

"This way," Omar said and walked towards the white building with our suitcases.

Jogging slightly to keep up, I looked around for something to show the physical boundary line between the two nations. The same bright glaring sun and the same open blue sky. The only thing different was the national flag.

"We leave this here and go check passport."

"Leave our luggage?" Emily asked. "Where?"

"Here."

I looked at the suitcases already there. "People just leave their luggage out here? Without anyone watching over it?"

"Yes, yes, is ok," Omar assured me.

"I'd rather take them with us."

"No, no is ok. No one take them."

"We really shouldn't leave luggage alone," I insisted.

Omar put his hands up. "Okay, okay." He turned to a soldier standing nearby and spoke in rapid Arabic.

"He will watch your suitcases," he said with a smile.

"Um… Thank you," I answered. A military guard was not quite what I had in mind, but it seemed it would have to do.

Glancing over my shoulder several times, I followed Emily and Omar into the white building to have my passport and visa checked. Then we retrieved our luggage from the soldier who was still guarding them, and went through luggage check.

"Omar," I whispered as the inspector opened my suitcase. "I have a lot of things from Israel. Jewish religious things. Is that allowed?"

Omar laughed. "Is ok. Many people cross to Jordan from Israel and bring souvenirs. Relax!"

Heart thudding, I watched the officer search through my clothes, underwear, toiletries, and souvenirs.

Please don't find the kippas, please don't find the kippas....

The officer picked up the paper bag stuffed full of beautifully embroidered skull caps with the Star of David on them. They were gifts I had bought for my friend's children, whose father is an orthodox Rabbi.

Barely glancing inside, he placed the bag in my suitcase and closed it. He asked Omar some questions and then we were free to go.

"Now we wait here for taxi." Omar waved his arm toward a little hut with no door. "Go inside in shade. I wait here with others."

The little hut was already full of people and all the chairs being used by a large Jordanian family, encompassing several generations and children, and the American tourists who were on the bus with us. With nowhere else to go, Emily and I stood in the back corner of the hut. A tiny, old TV was mounted on the wall and playing local shows, but no one was watching. The Jordanian family was gathered around an older woman wearing a black abaya. Reaching down, she opened the large esky at her feet and started pulling out sandwiches, packets of chips, sweets, juice boxes and cans of coke.

My stomach rumbled. Breakfast seemed like such a long time ago, but right now I would settle for a cool drink instead of the warm water in my bottle. Sighing, I sipped my water and distracted myself by watching the people in the hut. The Jordanian family had split; the men stood together a little apart from the women who sat on the chairs, chatting and looking after the children. They had two volumes; loud and louder. The Americans were sitting near the hut entrance, and for some reason the men kept pulling out their wallets and American dollars.

"It's so hot! Why isn't there an air conditioner in here?" One of the American women fanned herself with some paper.

"Can you get some water?" The other woman asked the men who were with them.

A blue taxi pulled up, crammed as many passengers as could fit in the car and drove off. The same taxi returned a while later to take another group of passengers. And again. And again, until the hut was practically empty.

Omar walked into the hut with a big grin. "Come on, our turn now." He grabbed our luggage and helped the taxi driver load it in the boot of the car. "He take us to my car. It is outside border crossing."

The taxi driver sped off, drove fast for about five minutes, screeched to a halt and said something to Omar that made him jump out of the car and run to the boot.

"Hurry! He has to go back for other passengers."

Grabbing my long scarf and backpack, I got out quickly and closed the door. As soon as Emily's door had banged shut, the taxi took off leaving us standing in a cloud of white dust.

"This my car." Omar waved his arm in the direction of a car parked on the side of the road. "I take you to hotel in Amman. Don worry, I have air-conditioning in car."

Emily smiled. "Air-conditioning sounds good. I can't believe how much hotter it is here than Israel. I mean, we've only just crossed the border."

Leaning back in the comfortable seat, I sighed in relief as cool air made its way towards the back of the car.

Emily leaned closer and whispered, "Should one of us sit at the front with him? It feels rude to sit at the back."

I shook my head. "I'm not sure if were allowed to sit at the front near a man who is not a family member. Better to play it safe and sit at the back, until we are more familiar with the local customs."

"You like music?" Omar grinned into the review mirror and put on American pop music from the 90s.

"I do, but I would much rather hear some traditional Bedouin music. Do you have any?"

"Really? You interested in hearing that?"

"Yes," Emily answered. "What's the point of coming to Jordan and not learning about the culture and history?"

Omar's grin was threatening to take over his face. "I think tourists always want pop songs. This very good."

Driving with one hand, he fumbled around in the glove box and pulled out a CD. "Okay! You want traditional Bedouin, I give you traditional music."

"That's better," I told him. "It's much more interesting."

"How far is it to the hotel?" Emily asked.

"Two hours. Your hotel is in capital Amman. Very nice hotel."

I shoved my long scarf behind my neck, settling in for a long car ride and looked out the window. The scenery was dry hilly terrain, and there was hardly any other cars around.

"Emily, look! Camels! And goats, but look at the camels! Emily?"

Omar chuckled. "Your friend has been sleeping for a while."

I turned to look. Emily's head was resting against the window, her eyes closed.

"Are those Bedouin camps?" I asked Omar.

"Yes. There are still Bedouins here. They prefer to live traditionally instead of city. You will see more as we drive."

"What road is this? It just keeps going and going with no other roads."

"King's highway," Omar said proudly.

A few houses began to dot the landscape, some simple and small, others large and elaborate.

"Omar, those houses look so European. Why do they look so different to the other houses we drove past?"

"These are for rich people. They like to build European

style to show they are rich. Other houses are how everyone else builds."

I laughed. "Seems to me wherever you go, the rich have to show off their wealth."

Omar chuckled and began singing along with the music.

The closer we got to the capital Amman, the more houses lined the street. We drove through poor looking neighbour-hoods, and richer areas with large villas and more expensive looking cars.

Omar slowed down and then stopped the car.

"Have we arrived? I'll wake Emily."

"No, not arrived. Is traffic."

I leaned to the side to look out the front of the car. Cars filled up any available space, blocking each other and forcing the traffic to a complete standstill. Some cars had even been parked on the other side of the road, and the men stood around smoking and chatting. One of the smokers was a tall, slim young man with the most vivid red hair and startling blue eyes.

"Omar, is red hair and blue eyes common in Jordan?"

"Hmm? Oh, that man? Yes, we have it sometimes." He continued humming along with the music from his CD.

My eyes scanned the crowd for other women. Whenever I am in unfamiliar territory, I always feel more comfortable if there are other women around but I couldn't see any standing outside with the men. Apart from a few women sitting in cars, Emily and I seemed to be the only women there. My stomach tightened. I would feel a lot more comfortable when we joined our tour group. The old saying is true – there is safety in numbers.

CHAPTER 14
GOLDEN CAGE

The traffic jam eventually moved and Omar pulled up in front of a large, cream coloured tower with multiple levels.

"Here is hotel. I take bags inside, and tour director will call you."

"Okay, thanks. Emily," I nudged her elbow. "Emily, wake up."

Yawning, Emily stretched her arms. "Did I fall asleep? Sorry! I didn't even realise."

"It's okay. We're at the hotel, Omar is getting our luggage out of the boot."

I climbed out and walked to the hotel entrance where Omar was handing over our luggage to a tall man and a short, dumpy woman with very bright red lipstick and nails.

"Backpack also," the woman told me.

I glanced at Omar who nodded and slipped off my backpack. The woman put it on a conveyor belt to be x-rayed, along with the luggage.

"Walk through metal detector," the tall man ordered.

Surprised, I looked at Omar who nodded and waved me forward with his hands.

I walked through and the woman with bright red lipstick scanned me with a hand held metal detector.

My lips pressed together.

This is ridiculous! There was less security checks crossing the border!

"Can I go now?" I asked the woman.

"Yes, yes." She stepped aside.

"What about my luggage?"

"Yes, you can take."

"Thank you."

I waited for Emily to be cleared by security and walked into the foyer.

"Wow!" I breathed.

Everything inside was decorated with gold trimmings. Cream coloured tiles with golden streaks, navy blue and gold striped couches with gold trims and tassels. Even the glass elevator going up was held together by a gold coloured frame.

"Look at that crystal chandelier! It's huge!"

The enormous chandelier dangled from a gold chain, right above the couches in the lobby area. I made a mental note not to sit under it. Just in case.

"I go now," Omar announced. "I see you again when you leave Jordan."

"Huh? But… I thought you were our tour guide… " I said.

Omar laughed. "No, no. I am driver. I pick up clients and take them to airport. You meet tour guide tomorrow. Very nice man. Bye bye."

"Bye bye," I echoed, with a weak wave and turned to the reception desk.

The young man behind it looked down at us, his shiny oiled back hair glistening slightly under the light.

"Welcome to Jordan," he said smoothly. "May I have your passports please?"

He tapped away at his computer for a minute. "I am afraid your room is not ready. Please rest in lounge, and your room will be ready in few moments. So sorry for inconvenience."

"No problem, we can wait in the lobby," Emily told him.

"Excuse me, who are those people?" I asked, pointing to the three very large portraits behind him of an older man, a young man and a beautiful young woman, all dressed in European style clothes.

The concierge's thin lips spread into a smile. "This is our former King Hussein. The young man is his son, our King Abdullah and his wife Queen Rania."

"I didn't know Jordan was a monarchy," I admitted, blushing.

"Yes. He is very good King. Very popular."

"Thank you," I smiled and walked over to the navy and gold couch.

A waiter in a very smart uniform appeared in front of us, presenting two cocktail glasses full of fruit smoothies on a silver tray.

"Thank you but we didn't order these," I told him. With the opulence of the hotel on display everywhere, I dreaded to think how much these drinks would cost.

"They are complementary Madam."

"Thank you very much," Emily said and picked up the glasses.

The waiter gave a small bow and walked away.

"I think we've landed in another five star hotel we couldn't afford in Australia." I sipped the fruit smoothie carefully, trying to look elegant and sophisticated enough for the place.

"I know. That's why I'm going to enjoy this experience while it lasts," Emily said.

The tall concierge from the reception desk walked over in a slow and dignified manner.

"Pardon Madam, there is a phone call for you at reception."

"Me? Are you sure?"

"Yes, it is for Madam Noor."

"But I don't know anyone in Jordan, and I've only just arrived. Who would be calling me?"

"It might be your parents," Emily suggested.

"I doubt it. I talked to them yesterday. Anyway, it must be in the middle of the night in Australia."

"Would Madam like me to take a message?"

"No it's alright, I'll take the call. By the way, you don't have to call me Madam."

The concierge gave a small bow and led the way back to the reception desk.

I hope nothing is wrong at home; I thought and picked up the receiver.

"Hello?"

"Good afternoon Madam. I am Ameer, the director of the tour. We spoke on the phone when you were in Tel Aviv."

"Ah, yes. Thank you for your help."

"You are very welcome. I hope the transfer went well?"

"Yes, it was fine." I blushed, remembering how we sat for hours waiting for our guide on the Israeli side of the border.

"I just wanted to welcome you to Jordan. I always welcome my clients when they arrive. Tomorrow morning your tour will start at 8 AM. Your tour guide is called Salah. He will pick you up from the hotel lobby and take you to several sightseeing spots along the way to Petra."

"Sounds great. How many people are in the tour group?"

"I am not sure what you mean. There is you and your friend."

"Yes, but how many other people will be joining the tour?"

"Well, another Australian girl will join you in Petra for the day. Miss Noor? Hello?"

"Sorry, I'm still here. I was just trying to understand. Are you saying that for the whole tour, Emily and I will be alone with the tour guide?"

"Yes but do not worry. He is a very good man and you

will be safe. If you have any problems or worries, you call me. You still have my number?"

"Yes. It's just, well, we thought we had booked a tour for Israel and Jordan together, and assumed that the tour group from Israel would continue travelling together in Jordan."

"Ah, no. The company you booked with sub contracts to local tour guides. I am the owner of this tour company in Jordan. Any problems at all, you just call me."

"Well … It's just … I mean, is it okay in Jordan for two women to travel alone with a man they don't know?"

"Of course! You will be very safe, I assure you. He is very good man. Anything else I can help with?"

"No, I guess not. Thanks for calling."

"Enjoy your tour of Jordan."

I placed the receiver down and bit my lip.

I don't like this.

The concierge adjusted some papers on the immaculately tidy desk and cleared his throat.

"Excuse me, your room is ready now. Here are your keys. Abed will take you to your room."

I turned to look where the concierge was pointing. A middle aged man in a red uniform stood holding a golden trolley with our suitcases on.

"Thank you," I accepted the keys and walked over to Emily. "Our room is ready."

"Where should I put these glasses?"

"On the table Madam, the waiter will come pick them up."

We followed Abed into the elevator. The glass box rose from the ground slowly, giving me an excellent view of the lobby and the rest of the hotel. In the centre was the lobby and giant chandelier, surrounded on all four sides by numerous bedrooms on multiple levels. A quick glance down into the lobby was enough to make me feel lightheaded. If I could find some stairs, I would not be taking this lift again.

The elevator doors opened smoothly and I stepped out

onto a luxurious, plush red carpet. The room number was a lovely mosaic plaque, the door dark and expensive looking.

Abed opened the door, placed our suitcases inside, and only left after receiving a tip.

"Can you believe this room?" Emily gushed. "It's the nicest room we've stayed in so far."

The thick red carpet, red silky curtains and bed covers, crisp white sheets and pillows gave the room a very opulent feel.

"It looks great, but what's that smell?"

Emily sniffed the air and crinkled her nose. "Stale smoke."

"Are you sure? They wouldn't allow smoking in the bedrooms."

"The cigarette packets in the goodies basket say otherwise."

"Are you serious?!" I walked over to the goodies basket on the desk and sure enough, a couple of cigarette packets sat among the packets of peanuts and biscuits.

The room stank. It had to be aired out, but the windows wouldn't open. It was as though they had been nailed shut, and no matter how much we pulled and pushed, they remained firmly shut. We gave up and sprayed our perfume everywhere.

"What was that phone call about? Was it your parents?" Emily asked, pressing the buttons on the remote control. The TV remained blank.

"Oh, yeah. I got distracted by the room and almost forgot to tell you. It was the tour director welcoming us to Jordan."

"That's nice of him." Emily pressed some more buttons.

"There's more. We're on our own with a tour guide in Jordan, except for one day when another Australian girl will join us at Petra."

Emily stared at me. "What do you mean on our own?"

I explained what Ameer had told me. Despite his assurances of being safe, I couldn't help feeling uncomfortable. The reality was that I was now in a Muslim country, and the

Western freedoms I enjoyed at home as a woman would not necessarily be the same here. To top it all off, we would be travelling alone with a stranger for days. From what I had seen of the country during the drive to the hotel, very few women were out in public. Was it really okay for us to travel with a strange man who was not our relative? What if he was a creep?

We had two options; cut the trip short and return home now, missing out on Petra, or meet the tour guide tomorrow and decide then. If I had been travelling alone, I would have immediately taken a taxi to the airport, but travelling with a friend made me feel safer. We decided to wait and meet our tour guide.

The hotel's restaurant wouldn't open for another few hours, so we decided to go for a walk before dinner. Omar had told us we could wear Western clothes because Amman was quite modern and relaxed, so we swapped long skirts and scarves for long tunics over leggings and running shoes. To get to the actual city of Amman we would have to hire a taxi but we were too tired to explore the city on our own. We decided to walk around the neighbourhood instead.

OUTSIDE THE HOTEL gates the left sidewalk ended immediately and opened onto a main street with speeding cars and no pedestrian crossing. To the right, the street continued but didn't look very appealing. It looked like it only led to a residential area.

I turned back to ask the female security guard for directions.

"Excuse me, we want to go for a walk but there don't seem to be sidewalks to walk on. Which way should we go?"

She raised her dark eyebrows. "Walk?"

"Yes, a walk."

"Where?"

"I don't know yet. What is there to see around here that is not too far from the hotel?"

"Why are you going for a walk?"

"Huh? We like to walk."

"Why?"

Why?! Was she serious? Didn't people go for walks around here? What was so strange about wanting to go for a walk?

I didn't know how to respond. Walking is one of the best ways to explore a new place and meet the locals. "It's a good exercise," I said.

She looked at her male partner who shrugged his shoulders. Her long, bright red fingernail pointed to the location of the hotel on the map.

"Turn right."

"Okay, thank you."

We turned right and walked along the narrow footpath. Right next to the hotel was the Peruvian embassy, barely visible behind a tall stone wall and strong iron gates. On the other side of the street was a very large villa with a dog chained by the neck in the front garden.

The instant his eyes locked on us, the dog began pulling at his chain and barking fiercely.

If we wanted to continue walking, our only option was to cross the narrow street and turn left. This would take us very close to the dog, and he was starting to sound hoarse from barking. The other option was to turn back to the hotel. We chose the hotel. The poor dog was already distressed enough with us across the street. I worried that if we crossed to his side, he might just strangle himself trying to get at us. Better to go back.

So our walk lasted a total of 3 minutes.

The female security guard smiled slightly. "Oh you're back. That was quick."

I blushed. *Why do I feel like I've proven her right about something, without even knowing what it is?*

"We were worried about getting lost."

Without waiting for a reply, I hurried inside.

We went back to our room and tried to turn on the television but it stayed blank. With nothing else to do, we went downstairs to the lobby and watched the other guests for entertainment.

DINNER WAS a large buffet of European dishes covered with a silver lid. Although well cooked and part of a large selection, the flavours failed to explode in my mouth like the fresh food at the Kibbutz in Israel. Slightly disappointed, I returned to our shared room. The room still stank of smoke and the TV refused to turn on. Bored, frustrated and grumpy, I went to bed early wishing I was back in the Old City.

CHAPTER 15
TOURIST TOWN

Breakfast was a selection of sausages, eggs, tomatoes, hash browns and other things dripping with oil. Lighter options included fruit, yoghurt and juice. After spending two weeks in Israel, with fresh salads and vegetables served at every meal, the food at this hotel seemed heavy and greasy.

I finished my tea and pushed the plate away.

"It's almost 8.30," Emily said looking at her watch. "Our tour guide will be here soon."

"Better bring our luggage down."

My stomach tightened.

If he turns out to be sleazy or creepy, how will we tell him we don't want to go on the tour? Would he even care? We've already paid and it's not like we're asking for our money back. What if he gets upset or offended? I hate socially awkward situations.

Emily opened the door. Apart from the slept in beds, the room was exactly as it had been when we checked in. There was no point unpacking our suitcases for one night. Quick check that we hadn't left anything behind, and we went down to the lobby.

A chubby man with a big smile was waiting in front of the reception desk.

The tall concierge from yesterday gestured towards us with his hand. "This is Miss Noor and Miss Emily."

The chubby man pushed up his glasses and opened his arms wide. "Welcome to Jordan! Welcome! I am your tour guide. My name is Salah. Very happy to meet you Madam Emily and Madam Noor."

"Likewise," Emily said, "but you don't need to call me Madam. Just Emily is fine."

"Me too. Just call me Noor."

"No, no! I can't do that! Very disrespectful."

"No, really, we insist. We're just ordinary people," Emily said.

"Madam makes me feel old," I told him with a smile.

Salah laughed and put up his hands. "Okay, okay Miss Noor."

I laughed. "Really, just Noor is fine. You don't need to call me Miss."

Salah's closely shaven head bobbed up and down. "Very well Miss Noor. Sorry!"

Emily laughed.

"If there is anything you need, please tell me. We have small tour group this time so you are boss. We go as slow as you want. I take your bags to car."

"Um, sorry – just a minute. Are you sure it's okay for us to travel alone with you?" I asked.

"Yes, definitely. We have lots of tourism in Jordan and tourist police. You will be very safe, I promise. Also, I am very happily married man with three children." He held out his phone with a picture of his family.

"You have cute kids," Emily told him.

His smile got even bigger. "Yes but they are very naughty."

Emily looked at me and nodded once.

I was torn. Emily felt comfortable enough with him to go on the trip, but I always err on the side of caution. My cautious side told me to go to the airport. My adventurous side insisted on seeing Petra.

He doesn't seem suspicious, and we are travelling in two so it's much safer than travelling alone, I told myself.

I nodded back to Emily.

"Ready to start tour?" Salah asked, still smiling.

I've never seen anyone so cheerful.

"Sure," Emily answered.

"Okay, I take bags to car. This way please."

Salah opened the boot and loaded our luggage, then dashed to the back door and opened it for Emily. "I open door for you Miss Emily. Is part of the service."

"Oh, you don't need to do that."

"No, I insist. I am your tour guide and driver. I open doors for you. Wait a minute Miss Noor! I open door for you."

My hand froze on the door handle. "It's okay, I can open it myself. I always do back home."

"Miss Emily," he indicated with his hand to the car seat.

Emily looked at me with a bemused smile and sat in the car. Salah closed the door and rushed over to my side. Resistance was futile.

"Okay ladies, we go at your pace." Salah turned the engine on and drove out of the hotel car park. "First we visit Madaba where they have beautiful Mosaics, then I take you to Mount Nebo where Moses saw the Promised Land. Then we visit old Kerak Fortress and then Ain Musa, where Moses hit rock and it gave water. Many people visit it and drink from water. Very pure water, very nice. Some say it has healing powers."

"We're seeing *all* that today?" Emily asked.

"Yes, on our way to Petra. We stop anytime you like so tell me when you are tired."

"When will we reach Petra?" I asked.

"Late this afternoon. Is very easy drive down Kings Highway. You sit back, relax and enjoy. I put on music for you if you like."

"Sure, but play some traditional music," I told him.

Salah's head bobbed from side to side. "Okay Madam! Sorry! Miss Noor!"

I shook my head but was smiling. "Just Noor."

SALAH WAS true to his word. He let us take as long as we wanted admiring the mosaic map of the ancient world at Madaba. He didn't rush us as we shopped for souvenirs at a mosaic factory set up by Queen Noor of Jordan to employ women and people with disabilities. When we stared nostalgically at Israel from the viewing point on Mount Nebo, Salah patiently waited near the car. During a rest break in a small village, he offered to buy water and snacks on our behalf so we wouldn't be charged tourist prices. At the Crusader Castle Kerak, Salah explained the history and told us to explore as long as we like. It was the best of both worlds – independent exploring and guided tour.

"Bit different from travelling with Mahmud," Emily joked, carefully making her way down the stone steps.

"You can say that again. Salah has got to be the most laid back tour guide I've ever met."

"Oooh! It's so lovely and cool in there!" Emily whispered over her shoulder and walked through the doors.

"Bit smaller than I expected." I was hoping the Kerak Castle artefacts exhibit would be a bit larger, but at least it was well presented.

A young woman with her hair covered by a pink head-scarf wandered around aimlessly. If it hadn't been for the staff ID card around her neck, I would have mistaken her for a tourist.

"Is that -? No! Can't be! Do they realise what they're listening to?"

"What are you talking about?" I asked Emily.

"Listen to the song. Do you recognise it?"

Pop music played loudly from the speakers around the room. "You can brush my hair, undress me everywhere…"

I gasped and smothered my giggles.

Emily was trying hard not to laugh, and failing.

I lowered my hand, eyes wide. "Do they know what it means? Undress me everywhere?"

Emily shrugged her shoulders and tried to put on a serious face. It was very hard concentrating on the artefacts with the song playing in the background, so we gave up and returned to the car where Salah was waiting with a smile.

"You ladies have fun? I turn air-conditioning in car for you."

"Thanks," Emily said and slid into the back seat with a cheeky grin before he had a chance to open the door for her.

"Salah, do many Jordanians know English?" I asked as he opened the door for me.

"Not all, but many work in tourism and know English. Why?"

Laughing, I told him about the song's lyrics which sent him and Emily into a fit of laughter.

"They probably don't understand what words mean," he said.

"Where to next?" Emily asked.

"Now is long drive to Petra but we stop for lunch and rest break along the way. Before Petra we visit one more place – Ain Musa, Well of Moses. Ah, yes! I almost forget to tell you. Petra has a special night tour. Is very, very special experience but I won't tell you or will ruin surprise. They only do this special tour at night. It has to be dark. If you want to go, I have to book tickets when we get to the hotel."

"What do you think?" Emily asked me.

"We'll still get to see Petra during the day, won't we?" I asked Salah.

"Of course! This is extra, and is not included in the tour."

"Is it safe to go to Petra at night?"

"Yes, yes. Many, many tourists go. And I will take you

there, wait for you and take you back to hotel so you will be safe."

"Okay, if you're sure it's safe …"

Salah nodded. "I will book for you."

We passed the time chatting about our families, comparing cultural practices and telling jokes. Apart from the occasional Bedouin camp with herds of goats and camels, we didn't see anyone else until we stopped for a rest break at a makeshift café by the side of the road. A young teenage boy ran out to offer us a steaming cup of hot tea with a fresh mint leaf in it, which was surprisingly refreshing in spite of the heat. I had barely finished drinking mine when Salah urged us back into the car to continue the long, long drive.

"Better wake Miss Emily. We are at Ain Musa."

"I'm awake." Emily stretched and took off her sunglasses.

"We are in Wadi Musa, the Valley of Moses," Salah explained. "We go inside to see the spring and you can drink from it or wash your hands and face."

The building was a small, white washed, multi domed structure. Inside was even plainer. At one end of the rectangular room was the rock Moses had struck for water. The spring of water had been almost completely covered by a brick floor, with a rectangular pool in the centre, with some steps leading down to it.

Apart from two young men washing their faces in the rectangular pool, we were the only ones there. Salah greeted them and they chatted for a minute before the young men stood and left.

"Did we interrupt them?" I asked. "We can wait outside for them to finish."

"No is okay, they finished. I wait for you outside. Take your time."

The water was surprisingly crisp and cool but I didn't dare drink it. Instead, I splashed it on my face and the back of my neck. It was incredibly clear and you could see it running through the room, under the brick floor and out of the building. Not wanting to keep Salah waiting long, we took a few photos and hopped back into the car. There was still a bit of a drive to reach Petra.

"Salah, are these all hotels?" I asked, looking around the small town from the car window.

"Yes, this is very much tourist town full of hotels."

"Why is it so empty? It looks like a ghost town."

"Tourism is bad now. When there are problems in the Middle East, people are afraid to travel. It is very safe in Jordan, but problems in other countries affect our tourism. The war in Syria has made people very nervous to come to Middle East."

Not just affected. It looks like it decimated the tourism here.

Everywhere I looked was empty building and streets.

Salah pulled up in front of the hotel we were staying in.

It was enormous.

Like the hotel in Amman, we had to present our luggage to be scanned before entering into a lobby as big as my entire house in Melbourne, backyard included. The floors seemed to be made of marble, the couches and armchairs had a silky finish with gold embroidery, an antique looking wood bar stood proudly in the corner, potted plants brightened the room and the balcony offered a breathtaking view of Petra.

The only thing missing was people. No concierge, no hotel guests, no hotel staff. The Jordanian Royal family, wearing Western style clothes, smiled down on us from their portraits hanging above the reception desk. Salah rang the bell on the desk and the concierge appeared, immaculately dressed in a crisp white shirt, tie and vest. Like the concierge at the hotel in Amman, he was also very thin and tall, his dark wavy hair smoothed back.

"Welcome to Jordan and Petra," the concierge said in perfectly pronounced English with a hint of an accent. "I hope you enjoy your stay here in our hotel."

Salah started talking to him in an Arabic dialect which I could not understand, so I waited for him to translate.

"I am sorry Miss Emily and Miss Noor, the hotel cannot offer you the usual buffet dinner tonight because you are the only guests. But chef can make whatever you want."

"Only guests?" I tried not to sound too alarmed. "What do you mean we're the only guests?"

"We are expecting more guests late tonight, but you are the only ones here for dinner," the concierge explained. "It's been a very quiet tourism season. If you tell me what you would like to eat, I will inform the chef."

"I usually have a light dinner, maybe some salad or falafels if you have any," I said.

"I don't mind as long as it's vegan," Emily said.

"What is vegan?" The concierge asked.

"Nothing with meat or any animal products. No eggs, no honey, no yoghurts or milk or cheese. I'll be happy with a salad," Emily told him.

"What time shall I tell chef to have dinner ready?"

"Um, well, not sure... I mean, whenever he is ready," I babbled.

I wasn't accustomed to ordering a dinner time from a chef.

"Sorry Miss Emily and Miss Noor, dinner will have to be at seven because we have to leave by eight PM for the night tour of Petra," Salah interjected.

"Very well, I will tell chef 7 PM. Is there anything special you would like to eat?"

"Hommous," Emily said and I grinned.

"I was just about to suggest that," I said.

The concierge handed us our keys and explained the direction to find our room and the dining room. The directions were rather complicated; we had to enter a lift and go down to level 1 where the pool was (the hotel had at least 5 levels of extensive floors with many, many empty rooms), and then walk down a long and winding corridor, take a left and walk on until we reached the next set of lifts that would take us down to the level of our room.

The lifts and hallways were empty like the rest of the

hotel. No noise, no sound of human voices, and because we were now underground, (the hotel was built into the cliff-side of a small hill) there was no natural sunlight. Even worse, only a few lights were turned on so we mostly walked in the dark. It felt like walking around in a huge, empty tomb, and despite the enormous size of the place I felt like I was suffocating. For the first time during the trip, I was glad I had to share a room with Emily. What had been a cost saving technique, might now become a lifesaver. There was no way I was sleeping in this ghostly hotel on my own.

Emily opened the door and gasped. "Look outside! The sun is setting over Petra!"

"Where? Damn, where's my camera when I need it?!"

I rushed to the balcony after her and stood in the cool breeze.

The sun turned a deep red and slowly sank into the moun-tainous terrain, its rays caressing the rock city nestled in the horizon.

It was breathtaking.

"NOOR, you better hurry up and get changed. We have to go to dinner."

"Already? Where has the time gone?"

"You've been staring at that sunset for at least 10 minutes," Emily said and laughed.

She had already changed into more practical clothes and proper walking shoes.

"I packed the flashlights and extra water bottles for us," she pointed to the bulging backpack on the bed.

"Thanks, I'll just be a minute." I grabbed my clothes and ran into the bathroom to change my long skirt to leggings and a long tunic. It was very difficult trying to dress modestly and stay cool at the same time.

The dining room was about as easy to find is our room

had been. I couldn't believe this hotel had so many corridors and stairs. It was like being in an underground maze.

"This must be the dining room," Emily said.

A good looking young man with wavy chestnut hair and very vivid green eyes opened the glass door. He was wearing a similar uniform to the concierge, with the addition of a vest.

"Good evening ladies, I am Karam the Butler."

"Hello Karam, I am Emily and this is Noor."

Karam bowed. "Welcome to Jordan, I hope you enjoy your stay in Jordan and our hotel. You are very welcome here." He stepped back slightly and swept his arm across the large empty dining room. "You may sit anywhere you like. All the tables offer a view of Petra."

"A table not too near the windows?" I suggested. "It's still very bright outside."

"Certainly madam."

Karam led the way to a beautifully set table with a crisp white tablecloth, elegant glasses and silver cutlery. A young man wearing a similar uniform appeared next to Karam's elbow. "This is your waiter Yusuf. If there is anything you need or would like, please tell us."

"Your English is incredibly fluent," I said.

"Thank you Madam."

"Please, just call me Noor."

"Noor is an Arabic name. Did you know it means 'light?' "

"Yes, I know." I smiled. "I'm actually half Italian and half Lebanese."

"Ah, now I understand. You look quite European and I didn't know how you could have an Arabic name. Welcome, welcome to Jordan."

"Thank you." I fidgeted in my seat.

I really should be used to this by now, it's not the first time they've made a fuss about my name in the Middle East.

"If it is all right, I will serve dinner."

"Yes, thank you. We are starving!" Emily said.

Karam clicked his fingers. Yusuf disappeared behind

silver doors and reappeared carrying a silver tray covered with a large silver lid. Karam picked up the cloth napkins on our table and draped them over our laps.

I blushed. While I enjoyed the comforts of five-star travel, only possible due to the currency conversion, I just couldn't enjoy people waiting on me hand and foot. It made me feel so pretentious.

Yusuf stood with one arm behind his back, holding out the tray for Karam to uncover.

The chef had gone above and beyond our request for salad and hummus. He had prepared a vegan feast.

"Wow! It looks amazing," Emily said and for the first time, Karam's professional butler face slipped and he grinned.

He set the plates on the table, poured our drinks and stepped back far enough to give us privacy but close enough to respond immediately if we called.

"This hotel must have been fabulous at one point," Emily said, carefully placing samples of each salad onto her plate. "It's definitely had a lot of money invested in it."

I looked around the enormous room, full of elegant wooden tables and chairs, crisp white linen and silver cutlery. "It just looks sad and empty now. Like a relic of the good old days."

"Oh my gosh, you have to try this bread. It's still warm!"

I grinned and filled my plate with hummous, the various salads and mouth-watering bread. It was so good we almost finished everything on the table.

I glanced over at Karam and he immediately glided over.

"Was everything to your liking?"

"Yes, definitely. Everything was delicious," Emily told him. "Please pass our compliments to the chef."

Karam smiled. "The chef will be most happy to receive your compliments. Tomorrow morning we will be able to serve you the full buffet breakfast. We are expecting guests to check in later tonight."

"Our tour guide told us it's been a very quiet tourist season in Petra," I said.

"Yes. It is the civil war in Syria. It makes people nervous to travel to the Middle East. A lot of this town was built as a response to a tourism boom, but now most of the hotels are empty."

"Hopefully the tourism season improves for you," Emily said.

"Thank you for a wonderful dinner." I stood and placed my napkin on the table.

Emily finished her drink and stood.

Karam's eyebrows rose, his brilliantly green eyes wide. "But, where are you going?"

"We're doing the night tour of Petra." Emily smiled. "Our tour guide is picking us up from the lobby."

"Thank you again for the delicious dinner." I padded my stomach. "I'm so full."

"But, but… You haven't finished your dinner!"

"Yes we have." I pointed to the table. "We've eaten almost everything."

"That's only the entree. The chef has prepared the main meal and desert for you."

"Oh, I'm so sorry. I thought that was the meal. We asked for a light dinner… "

"Yes, we know. The chef has prepared a light dinner. Only some grilled chicken and vegetables for you, and roast vegetables for Miss Emily. That is vegan, right?"

Emily slowly sat back down and smiled weakly. "Yes, that is vegan."

Karam held out my chair.

"I guess I could eat a little more…"

When he had made sure we were seated with the napkins on our laps, Karam snapped his fingers and Yusuf brought out the main meal. As full as I was, I had a little room left for the sumptuous, soft chocolate sponge cake.

Karam was hovering nearby and I was getting a little

anxious he would ambush us with another course. If I ate any more I would have to waddle through Petra.

"That was delicious, and I couldn't possibly eat another mouthful," Emily stood up and started edging towards the door.

"If I eat any more, I'm going to explode."

"You are most welcome!" Karam said with a big grin. "Is there anything else we can get you? Some tea and coffee? Perhaps with some biscuits to nibble on?"

"No! I mean, thank you but we are so full," I said, backing out of the dining room.

"You've been very hospitable," Emily thanked him and nodded at Yusuf. "We really have to get going now, our tour guide will be waiting for us."

"Yes, can't be late for Petra."

"Very well ladies," Karam said and bowed slightly. "Enjoy your night tour of Petra and we will see you in the morning for breakfast.

CHAPTER 16
CITY OF CAVES

The ten minute drive to Petra took us through the small winding roads of the local village. The locals were enjoying the cool evening breeze on their balconies, sipping coffee and chatting with their friends.

Salah stopped the car in front of a gate. "Here are your tickets. Did you remember your flashlights? Good. I will pick you up from here after the tour. I'll just be waiting out here with the other tour guides. Security will not let you into Petra until it is dark, but we needed to get you a bit early so they can check your tickets."

"I didn't realise the night tour would be so popular," I mentioned, stepping out of the car.

"Yes, it is very popular. But this is a bad season for tourism," Salah lamented.

I looked at the crowd of 100 or more people from all over the world. I could already hear some British, American, European and Latin American accents. There was also a large number of Asian tourists.

"Enjoy the tour," Salah waved and drove off.

The guards checked everyone's tickets but didn't open the gate. The crowd's chattering lowered to a hum. Everyone was watching the light fade, waiting for the sky to darken.

I pulled out my flashlight and waited.

The guard stepped up to the gate and pushed it open.

We began to move, almost as one body, through the gates and into Petra.

"Wait," I whispered to Emily. "We forgot to ask Salah for a map!"

"I don't think it matters," Emily whispered. "Just follow the crowd. I heard someone say we're going to the Treasury."

The pathway was narrowing, forcing the loosely dispersed crowd into marching lines. A small flickering light on the ground caught my eye. And another. And another after that. A long, sneaking path of little lights that continued endlessly into the darkness.

I leaned down for a closer look. A brown paper had been filled with sand and nestled one small tea light candle. Quite romantic but not very pragmatic. I turned on my flashlight and pointed it to the ground covered in small rocks and pebbles.

"I bet you're glad we bought proper walking shoes," Emily commented.

"Yep. And water." I took a long swig from my bottle. "I can't believe it's still so hot."

"Save some for later. Apparently it's a one hour walk to the Treasury. And we have to walk back."

I grimaced and focused on where I was putting my feet.

We walked and walked.

The pathway to the Treasury narrowed, forcing us to walk in single file.

Sweat dripped down my face.

I looked up but there was no sign of the stars. Darkness. A deep, oppressive darkness.

The stone walls closed in around me. The passage was so narrow I could touch both sides easily by slightly extending my arms.

If it gets any narrower, I won't be able to go through.

"Almost there," Emily said over her shoulder. "I can see the exit."

I didn't look up. The uneven ground was full of small stones that could easily trip me. The last thing I wanted was to hobble out of Petra on a twisted ankle.

Emily gasped and her flashlight went out.

My head snapped up.

"Emily?" I waved my flashlight around. "Where are you?"

"Come through."

I stepped into the darkness, squeezing through the narrow gap.

"Oh!"

Hundreds and hundreds of little flames flickered softly, their warm glow illuminating the Treasury. Most of the group had already arrived and was sitting on the ground.

"There's a free mat over there," Emily whispered. "Pity we're right at the back."

I followed her to the dusty mat. "There's more coming. Ouch!"

"What's wrong?" Emily whispered.

"I think I sat on something." I lifted up the edge of the mat and brushed aside the small sharp rocks.

"Poor thing," Emily mumbled distractedly, trying to take a picture of the Treasury.

Bedouins carrying trays full of cups walked between the rows of tourists. My water bottle was still half full but I couldn't resist the steaming cup of tea when it was offered.

Blowing softly into my cup, I gazed at the Treasury. I could hear Emily chatting quietly to the girl sitting next to her about all the usual things travellers ask each other; where are you from? Where have you been? Isn't this great?

I sipped the sweet tea, mesmerised by the flickering candle lights. The air was thick with anticipation. Everyone was looking straight ahead and talking in hushed voices.

Excited murmuring broke out. I looked over at Emily who was using the tone she normally reserved for cats.

"What the –? Where did they come from?"

Two cats had made themselves comfortable on the laps of Emily and the girl next to her. More cats were wandering between the rows of tourists and choosing a human to sit on. A wave of homesickness washed over me. Both of my fur kids like to sit on my lap, with a slight difference that Bruli is a 40 kg Rhodesian ridgeback while Susu is a very cuddly and sometimes grumpy old cat.

"Isn't he gorgeous?" Emily gushed over the cat that was happily snoring on her legs.

The girl next to her was patting the cat curled on her lap. "I love cats!"

That was enough for Emily to start a conversation with the girl about their mutual love of cats until a couple of Bedouins stood at the front of the group and started playing traditional music. I couldn't see what instruments they were using or where the singing was coming from but in a way it made the whole experience more magical.

I was transfixed and when the singing ended the crowd stood reluctantly. Except for Emily's new friend. Every time the poor girl tried to stand, the cat dug its nails into her legs. The others near us laughed and took pictures. Emily had managed to gently shift her cat onto the ground and very reluctantly bid him good night.

"We better head back," I told her. "It's a long walk and Salah will be waiting for us."

"I wish I could take him back with me."

"You wish that about all the cats we've met on this trip." I laughed. "I hope this hotel has better Wi-Fi than the last one."

My sister had promised to keep me updated with stories and photos of my little Bruli and Susu, and tonight's encounter with the Petra cats had made me miss them even more.

Emily wished her new friend good luck and good night and we headed back through the narrow passageway, following the candle path back to the gate. This time though, I was being guided by a bright light at the end of the tunnel – quite literally. The tourist office at the entrance of Petra was shining so brightly we didn't need our flashlights. It was already late and by the time we got to the hotel, found our room and washed off the dust, I could barely keep my eyes open.

THE NEXT MORNING Salah picked us up early from the hotel and drove to Petra. He parked the car as close to the entrance as he could, but we still had to walk several minutes before reaching the ticket gate.

"Ah, here is Sarah. She is also Australian like you but from Brisbane. Excuse me, I need to answer this phone call." Salah moved slightly away, talking loudly and cheerfully into the phone.

"Hi, nice to meet you. I'm Emily and this is Noor."

"Hi, nice to meet you guys."

I smiled and gave a small wave hello, slightly distracted by the group of horses standing near the ticket gate. Their riders were young Bedouin men laughing and joking with each other loudly. Some of the horses lowered their heads only to have them immediately pulled back up high by their rider. One of the young men kicked his horse into a gallop, smacking the long leather reins across its flanks to make it run faster across the hard ground. They galloped several hundred metres before turning around and returning to the ticket gate.

"That horse is lame. He shouldn't be running."

"How do you know?" Emily asked Sarah.

"I keep horses back home."

My lips pressed together tightly. I could see the shape of the rib cage on several of the horses.

Salah hung up and walked back towards us with a smile. "If you like, you can ride on horses to the Treasury but I think it is nice to walk. You see more and I have many things to show you."

"I would rather walk," I said quickly.

"Me too," Emily said.

Salah looked at Sarah who nodded.

"Okay, we walk. Maybe I lose some weight," Salah joked and we laughed politely. "I am sorry to start so early, but it gets very hot here. Better to walk now in the morning. First I will take you to look at cave houses and then we continue walking to the Treasury. After that, we explore the city and if you want to you can walk up to the Temple."

"Sounds good," Sarah said and Emily nodded.

Salah smiled cheerfully. "Follow me."

I slipped my sunglasses on and adjusted my hat. Even though it was early, the sun was already very bright and warm. Last night had been too dark to see Petra but in the morning light everything was laid bare. The sand and dirt are almost white in colour and everything is incredibly dry.

"Look here ladies," Salah waved his arm at a shrub growing down the side of the rocks. "Even though there is no water, nature is amazing, no?"

I grinned and took a photo of the solitary, resilient green plant.

"Come up here but please be careful not to slip. Be very careful, I don't want anyone to fall. These are the caves that Bedouins used to live in before the Jordanian government moved them to a settlement close by in the 1980s."

"Why?" I asked.

"That's when they turned Petra into a tourist destination. Tourism brings in a lot of income for Jordan. But don't worry, the government gave them all brand new houses and many of them come to work in Petra every day just like they used to. They make souvenirs for tourists and take them through Petra on horses or camels."

"Families really used to live in here?" Sarah asked. "It looks so small from the outside."

"Yes, yes. The whole family would live in these cave houses. Let's go in this one and I'll show you."

I followed the others through the opening and sighed in relief. It was so lovely and cool, like sitting in a room with an air conditioner.

"Look up at ceiling. See the black marks? That is from fire from cooking."

My eyes looked past Salah's finger to the exquisite colours in the stone. Various shades of turquoise blues and pink darkening into purple decorated the roof and walls in swirling patterns. A ray of sunlight slipped in and the colours sparkled. It was breathtaking.

"Very interesting story about Petra," Salah said. "A woman who is your neighbour, from New Zealand, married a Bedouin man and lived here until the government moved them to the new settlement. Her son works here. They make jewellery inspired by Petra and sell to tourists. He speaks English with Kiwi accent. I take you to meet him."

I grinned. "You know what a 'Kiwi' accent is?"

Salah laughed. "The son told me. I noticed his English had a different accent to Americans and Australians, and English too. His mother has the same accent, and he studied in New Zealand for a few years."

"Can we meet her too?" Sarah asked.

"Yes, I'd love to hear about her life story," Emily said. "It's so interesting."

"I don't know if she is there. Sometimes she is there and sometimes her son works there. But I know she wrote a book about her life and you can buy it at their stall."

"I'm definitely buying the book," I said.

"Me too," Emily said. "And looking at the jewellery."

Grinning, I followed the others out of the cave house.

Salah led the way through the valley, cheerfully talking about the history of Petra. I had given up on concentrating. His words blended together in the heat and glare of the merciless sun.

"Move, quick!" Salah threw out one arm and frantically waved the other one. "Over here!"

Slightly dazed, I looked at the others flattening themselves against the rocks.

The thundering sound behind me got louder. The sound of a whip hissing through the air jolted life in my limbs. I rushed to the rocks where the others had taken shelter and pressed my back against the cool stone. A scrawny horse galloped towards us, dragging a small carriage full of people. His owner was flicking a whip and clicking his tongue while the overweight family lounged in the seat.

"We need to be careful or we will be run over," Salah joked but no one laughed.

"Do the horses get rest breaks?" I asked. It was the most diplomatic way I could think of to ask if they were well treated.

"Of course, when there are no tourists they rest."

Emily pressed her lips together and Sarah didn't look much happier, but what could we do apart from refusing to ride on the poor animals?

Deflated, I pulled out my bottle and gulped a mouthful. "Ugh! Gross, my water is hot!"

"Yes, is very hot today," Salah said. "There is cafe near Treasury and you can buy cold drink. We have break there and then continue walking."

I pushed myself off the rock, ordering my legs to move. My feet seemed to weigh more with each step. I gulped some more hot water and wiped the sweat off my forehead.

We walked, and walked and walked. Or maybe it was the heat playing tricks on me, making the path seem longer than last night.

"How much longer?" I croaked, leaning against a rock.

Any water I drank was immediately converted into sweat, leaving my throat dry and scratchy.

Salah looked over his shoulder and stopped walking, Emily and Sarah close behind.

"We are close. We are about to enter the Siq."

"The what?" I asked.

"Siq is – what you call it? Ravine? Is that word correct?"

Sarah and Emily nodded.

"It is like path, with stone walls and at the end it is only 1 meter wide. I hope I fit through!" He joked and the others laughed.

I managed a weak smile and finished the rest of my water. My legs felt weak and trembly, my heart was pounding and I was sweating buckets.

"Are you alright?" Emily asked, offering me a bottle of water from her backpack.

"Thanks." I drank a third of it and wiped my mouth dry. "I think I'm a bit dehydrated."

"Will you be ok?" Salah asked, not smiling for the first time.

"Yes, I'll make a hydrating drink when we get to the Treasury. That will help."

He nodded. "It will be cooler in the Siq, there is shade there."

"Oh good," I said. "Let's keep going. The sooner we get there, the happier I will be."

Salah nodded and led the way, followed by Sarah. Emily kept looking back over her shoulder as I trudged along slowly.

"Do you need to stop and rest?"

"I really need to get out of the sun. I might as well not be wearing a hat for all the good it's doing. I'll be okay in the shade."

"Okay," Emily said doubtfully. "We're almost there. I can see the entrance to the Siq."

I nodded and pushed on, reaching it in a few minutes. The relief was instant. In the shade, the temperature was slightly cooler and I could catch my breath without the sun beating down on my head.

The stone walls were so high they darkened the passage. I tipped my head back and could just see a slither of the vivid blue sky above.

If this is how dark it is during the day, no wonder it had been so black in here last night.

Salah was in front, sometimes humming and sometimes making jokes that required Emily and Sarah to chuckle politely. I couldn't remember how long the walk through the Siq was so I paced myself and plodded along. There was nowhere else to go in this stone tunnel so I didn't worry about losing sight of them. Just like last night, I kept my eyes mostly on the uneven ground. I lost track of time and just kept walking until I heard excited chatter ahead.

I raised my eyes from the loose stones on the ground and gasped.

A glimpse of the Treasury appeared through a gap in the narrow walls of the Siq. My feet moved faster and I stepped out of the ravine. Exquisitely carved into the rose hued stone, the Treasury stood proudly and majestically.

A crowd of tourists was already there, posing for photos and hiring camels with brightly coloured saddles to take them further into the stone city. I walked over to join Emily and the others at the makeshift café that had been built right in front of the Treasury. Salah ordered cold drinks for us and we sipped them under a colourfully woven cover. Across from the café was a group of camels, donkeys and horses with brightly coloured saddles either lying in the soft reddish sand or waiting for the next tourist to hire them. They were a pitiful sight, scrawny and tired looking.

"Hey!" Emily nudged me. "Isn't that the cat from last night? The one who sat on the Brazilian girl's lap?"

"Maybe? It was too dark to get a good look."

It seemed the cats that had joined us for last night's performance lived nearby because many were snoozing in shady spots or approaching tourists for a pat, which Emily and Sarah did. Smiling, I mixed the hydrating powder into the water bottle and drank.

"Feeling better?" Emily asked.

I nodded and stood. "The heat makes my blood pressure drop," I explained, walking over to

Salah and Sara.

"I take you to see the Bedouin with Kiwi accent," Salah said.

We followed him past the enormous rocks where the Treasury was carved and around the corner where a whole stone city lay bleached almost white under the bright sun. Salah walked us past makeshift Bedouins souvenir stalls lining and deeper into the city.

A few young Bedouin men started following us on their horses.

"Come ride Michael Jackson," one of them called out.

"What?" Emily asked looking around.

"My horse is called Michael Jackson."

"Why is he called Michael Jackson?" Salah asked.

The one in front of the group gave us a cheeky grin. "Only ladies like Michael Jackson."

His friends laughed and one of the others added, "This way only ladies want to ride him."

My eyebrows rose. "Ha!" I couldn't tell if it was a marketing technique or a pick up line.

Laughing, Salah shook his head and kept walking.

"Ride my horse," one of them called out. "He runs very fast. I show you?"

Without waiting for an answer, he galloped the horse several metres before returning.

"Ladies, do you want to ride horses?" Salah asked our little group.

We all shook our heads so Salah said something to the young men and they left with a wave.

Salah stopped a few more times to show us various tombs and ancient carvings before taking us to meet the young Bedouin man with a kiwi accent. He introduced us as neighbours from Australia and the young man chatted to us in English for a few minutes about the jewellery his mother made and his time living in New Zealand. The jewellery was creative and pretty but we barely looked at it. Instead, we all bought copies of his mum's autobiography about her life in Petra with the Bedouins. When the young Kiwi's friends stopped by for a visit, Salah said goodbye and took us to a newly built restaurant for refreshments.

I bought a couple of bottles of water and skipped the food. My stomach was just too queasy to be tempted by anything on the menu.

I fanned myself with the menu, half listening to Salah explain that the Monastery was even more spectacular than the Treasury and that it was originally used as Nabatean tomb.

"How far is the Monastery?" Sarah asked.

"Depends on how fast you walk, but at least 40 minutes."

I cringed.

"Oh, and it is up so you have to climb 800 steps. Or is it more?"

"What? 800 steps?" I groaned loudly. "I don't think I can make it …"

Emily frowned. "I don't like your colour. Your cheeks are very red but you look pale."

"I don't feel great," I admitted.

"You can rest here as long as you need to," Salah said. "I will be waiting down here if you can't make it to the Monastery and want to come back down."

"Have some more water," Emily suggested.

"It's not helping. I keep drinking water and hydrolyte but I feel really dizzy and nauseous."

"It might be heat-stroke," Sarah suggested.

"Don't force yourself to walk up to the Monastery if you don't feel up to it," Emily said.

I nodded, staring at the wooden table.

"Have rest here in the shade and maybe you feel better in few minutes," Salah suggested.

"Okay." My voice sounded miserable.

Half lying on the table, I cradled my head between my arms and closed my eyes focusing on taking deep breaths. My head spun and my stomach rolled. Salah chatted to Emily and Sarah about the incredible view from the Monastery.

I squeezed my eyes shut tightly, fighting back tears.

I can't believe I make it all the way to Petra only to have to turn back now!

As much as I hated to admit that, there was no point deluding myself. The others optimism was wasted. I had felt steadily worse all day. There was absolutely no way my body would be able to handle both the heat and strenuous walk up to the monastery. Slowly, I raised my head and looked at Salah who stop talking and smiled at me.

"Feeling better?"

"I'm really sorry to do this, but I don't think I can go up to the monastery. I still have to walk back to the entrance afterwards, and I just don't have the strength."

"Don't worry about it," Emily said. "There's no point pushing your body to its limits if you're too sick to enjoy the view. I'll go back to the hotel with you."

"What if you rest here in the shade until Emily and Sarah come back?"

I shook my head. "I think it's better if I go back to the hotel and rest. I'm really sorry about this," I said looking at Emily and Sarah. "I don't want to ruin the tour so please continue without me. I'll be all right once I get out of this heat and rest."

Emily shook her head. "No way I'm letting you go back on your own in this state."

"Please, I feel bad enough making you wait here for me. I'll be fine. You go ahead to the monastery and I'll see you back at the hotel."

"Are you sure?"

"Yes."

"I will take miss Emily and miss Sarah towards the monastery and then get the car and meet you at the ticket gate. I will take you to the hotel and come back for the others."

"It's okay, I can catch a taxi to the hotel."

"No, no. You are not well. I will take you and come back for miss Emily and miss Sarah. It will take them a long time to walk up to the monastery and back to the ticket gate so I have time."

"Thank you. And I'm so sorry for this trouble."

"No trouble at all."

"Yes, just feel better," Sarah said.

"Are you sure you will be okay on your own?" Emily asked again.

I nodded. "Take lots of pictures of the monastery for me."

"I can't bring the car in Petra," Salah said. "Will you be okay walking back to the ticket gate? We can hire a horse to carry you."

"I can manage," I said. "I remember the way and the Siq is shady so that will help."

"I am very sorry I cannot bring car inside Petra but I will bring it as close as possible to the entrance so you don't have to walk far where we parked."

I forced my lips into a smile. "I'll just buy one more bottle of water and start walking back. It's going to take me a while and I don't want to keep you waiting at the gate."

Salah put up his hands. "Please do not worry. I have lots of time and I don't mind waiting."

"Make sure you keep drinking water and taking rest breaks," Emily ordered.

"I will. Nice meeting you Sarah." I waved goodbye and headed inside the restaurant to stock up on water before starting the long walk back.

When I came out, the others had already left. I started making my way back slowly, stopping frequently to drink water and crouching for a few minutes in whatever small patch of shade I could find. Several times one of the young men from earlier would stop his horse and offer me a ride. I almost accepted but the horses drooping heads and visible rib cages stopped me each time. If the heat was affecting me this badly and I kept drinking water, how much worse were the poor horses feeling after being galloped around all day in the sun, often carrying overweight tourists? I just couldn't bring myself to add to their burden so I pushed on, leaning on the cool stone walls of caves and tombs when I could.

I was sitting on the ground in a small patch of shade staring at my empty water bottle when a very thin young girl with short dusty hair and old worn clothes walked up to me.

She murmured something over and over.

I shrugged my shoulders. "Sorry, I can't understand."

"Petra postcards, only one dineri. Lots of postcards, just one dineri. Only 1 dineri."

"Ah, well … yes, I suppose." What I really needed was more water, not postcards but her appearance was pitiful. None of the Bedouins I had seen so far were dressed so shabbily. I found the money and handed it over.

"God bless you!" She put the money away and held out her hand. "1 dineri."

"I already gave it to you."

"For my troubles. One more for my troubles. Very hard walking in sun carrying heavy bag."

Pressing my lips together I pulled out another note and gave it to her.

"God bless you! God bless you!"

"Thanks." I pushed myself off the ground and walked away with my pack of postcards.

All I wanted was to be back in the cool hotel room.

I lost track of time. My legs felt swollen and heavy, my head was spinning and my heart was beating too fast. When I spotted the entrance, tears formed in my eyes.

I made it!

The knowledge that I would soon be inside Salah's air conditioned car seemed to give energy to my weary limbs. I stopped to buy a bottle of cold coke at the entrance and gulped it down. Salah wasn't there yet so I waited under the shade of a makeshift souvenir stand and bought some bottles of coloured sand as a gift for my sister. Each one had a different design but how they managed to create the shape of camels and Palm trees with sand inside such small bottles was beyond me. The man assured me they were all hand-made in Petra.

"There you are! I worried you got lost."

I turned to look Salah. "I'm so sorry. Did I keep you waiting? I didn't see your car."

"No, it's okay. I just got here but I was worried about you because you're not well."

"It took me longer than I thought it would because I had to keep stopping to rest."

"Come, I have the air conditioning on in the car."

I followed him and slid into the back seat, sighing with relief. The difference in temperature was incredible and my body was responding. My breathing eased and my heart rate started to slow down. I went straight from the car to my hotel room, took my medication and collapsed on the bed.

"Noor? Are you okay?"

I blinked and lifted my head off the pillow. "Hey, you're back. Sorry, I think I fell asleep."

"Are you feeling better?"

"Yes, heaps. I think it was walking for so long in the heat. It must have dropped my blood pressure too low."

"You want to go and cool down by the pool before dinner? There's a nice breeze outside."

"Good idea. Did you take lots of pictures? Tell me what it was like."

"Well, pretty much the whole way up and down Bedouins kept trying to sell as souvenirs or convince us to ride donkeys. I have to say though, it was worth the climb. The view from up there is breathtaking and we stopped to have some delicious tea before walking back down."

I hid my disappointment with a smile and listened to her

talk about how great it had been. As frustrating as it was, I knew I had made the right decision to go back to the hotel. The last thing I wanted was to trigger an Addisonian crisis and have to fly back home instead of exploring the Wadi Rum desert tomorrow.

A group of six Italian men were already sunbathing by the pool when we got there. One of them had fallen asleep in the sun and turned an alarming shade of red.

"Hey, isn't that the same Italian group we saw at Petra today?" Emily whispered. "Why are they still wearing their big crucifixes?"

I looked out of the corner of my eye at the man closest to me. Sure enough, a large wooden crucifix was nestled in his hairy chest.

Smothering a giggle I nodded and picked up her camera. "Show me those pictures."

We spent the afternoon enjoying the cool breeze by the pool before stuffing ourselves at the buffet style dinner. The evening's entertainment, besides trying type and email home on a keyboard without the @ sign, was watching Jackie Chan's *Rush Hour* movie dubbed in Arabic. Petra had been as incredible as I had imagined and my only regret was having to turn back instead of climbing up to the monastery.

CHAPTER 17
TEA TASTES BETTER IN A TENT

Wadi Rum desert, with its soft shifting sands and occasional lone shrub, was determined to compete with Petra for the award of the hottest location. I glanced at my watch.

9.30 am. How can it possibly be so hot at 9.30 in the morning?

My skin felt tight and dry, even though I had already drank a two litre bottle of water. The car's air conditioning was either not working or no match for the desert's heat.

"Here we are," Salah said cheerfully from the driver's seat. "We watch short documentary now, then we go into desert on a jeep."

"More driving?" I muttered under my breath.

After an hour and a half in the car, I didn't particularly want to get into another one.

Salah parked and we stepped outside.

"Are you sure its ok for us to dress like this?" Emily gestured to our leggings, long tunics and hiking shoes.

"Yes, is fine," Salah waved his hands. "You are tourists on adventure in Wadi Rum."

I glanced at my bare arms.

Should I have worn a long sleeve tunic like Emily? Even her leggings are longer than mine...

Shaking my head, I followed them into the sand coloured building and into a room with a large projector. The group of Italians from Petra and the hotel were already there, sitting in a neat little row with their large wooden crucifixes on display over their t-shirts.

I said hello in Italian and joined Emily on the row behind them.

"Why aren't you chatting to them in Italian?" Emily whispered. "You barely spoke to them this morning at breakfast."

I shrugged. "There wasn't much to say. We're pretty much following the same itinerary."

The screen came to life and I tuned out. It was so cool in here and I was so tired.

Emily nudged me. "Hello sleepy head, it's over."

Smothering a yawn, I followed her out of the room. "I wasn't sleeping, just resting my eyes."

Salah was waiting with a big smile. "Are you ready to have a jeep adventure? Come, our driver is outside."

I slipped my sunglasses on before stepping out into the bright light.

"This is our driver Atallah."

A thin young man stepped forward and embraced Salah then nodded in our direction.

"This is our driver?" I asked Salah, eyeing his pimples and braces.

"Is he old enough to drive?" Emily asked.

"Of course!" The boy answered, head held high and sharp chin jutting out. "I am 20 years old. I've been driving for years!"

Emily blushed. "Wow, your English is great."

"Really? You look younger," I told him.

He shrugged. "It's the braces."

Salah laughed. "Don't worry, he is old enough to drive."

Atallah gestured at the car behind him. "This is our jeep. Climb in."

"But, there's not enough room for all of us." I was eyeing

the front of the jeep which only had a driver's seat and passenger seat.

"You sit in the back."

We walked towards the back of the jeep. Someone had built a metal frame and covered it with a brightly coloured cloth as a roof of some sorts. Matching cushions for our backs and bottoms were tied to the frame.

"You will have to climb in," Salah told us and demonstrated how.

Emily climbed up first and sat on the seat opposite Salah. I gripped the metal frame and hauled myself up, flopping down next to Emily. Atallah waved to the other drivers, who looked as young as him, and climbed into the front seat.

"Hold the frame," Salah told us. "It will be a bumpy ride!"

My fingers had barely wrapped around the warm steel before Abdullah took off. We bobbed up and down across the sand, clutching to the poles to stop ourselves falling out. The air was dry and I could feel the temperature rising, but the striped red cloth over our heads provided enough shade to stop us suffering from heat stroke.

Atallah drove deeper into the desert. The clear blue sky stretched endlessly above and rock mountains sprouted up from the sand. The jeep slowed down and stopped.

"Why are we stopping?" I asked Salah.

He grinned, his usually twinkling brown eyes hidden behind dark sunglasses. "We give you traditional make up demonstration, teach you how to make make-up from plants."

I laughed. "Wouldn't it be more useful to teach us how to find water in the desert?"

Salah laughed and jumped out. "Come on, this is fun. The make-up is natural and organic and made in Bedouin tradition. Careful, watch your step."

Emily climbed over the back of the jeep gracefully. I swung one leg over, then the other, and jumped down.

Atallah had joined us and was chattering to Salah who nodded and beckoned us with his hand.

"First, we show you how to make soap. The Bedouin make it from this plant, and you add a little water like this – see? And now you have soap to wash hair and clothes. You try."

Emily and I took turns trying to make soap from the leaves of a plant whose name I couldn't remember. Then we tried making blush by grinding red stones into a fine powder, mixing it with a drop of water and tapping it onto our already red cheeks. Demonstration over, Atallah pointed out carvings of camels on the facades of these smallish rock mountains and offered to take our pictures if we wanted to climb up some of the smaller rocks. The fun part was walking in the sinking sand to try and reach the rocks. I could feel sand seeping into the breathable material of my shoes and almost lost my balance several times, much to the other's amusement.

"Last picture," Salah said from behind the camera. "We need to keep moving. Now we take you to ride a camel and then we have tea in Bedouin tent."

"Ooooh! I've never ridden a camel before!"

"I think I'll pass," Emily commented. "They're too high."

"Ah, yeah, I didn't think of that. Salah, if we don't want to ride, can we just pat them?"

"Sure, of course you can."

More than my fear of heights, I was thinking of the camels I had seen at Petra. As much as I would like to experience riding a camel in the desert, I wasn't going to if the camel looked tired, scrawny or badly treated.

Atallah flew the jeep over the sand, with the three of us clutching the frame and laughing. It was almost like an amusement park ride. He stopped the car in the middle of nowhere where a dark skinned man wearing a long, white flowing gown sat next to his camels.

He stood and walked over to Atallah and Salah. "Salam alaikum."

The men greeted each other and Salah pointed at me. "She can speak a little Arabic. Her mother is Lebanese. Ibrahim is from Sudan and he can speak Arabic like you."

"Marhaba," I said.

"Ahlan wusahlan *(Welcome)*."

"So, you want to ride the camels?" Salah asked.

I looked over at the two camels relaxing on the warm sand. They looked well fed.

"It's okay, I don't want to wake them up."

Ibrahim laughed loudly. "Is okay, they sleep all morning. Come, sit on them while they are on ground."

"I don't know," Emily hesitated. "Camels are very tall. I'll wait here for you."

"Come on, you'll be fine," I told her. There was something about the vastness and emptiness of the desert that was making me feel adventurous. "Here, you can ride the one in front so you can see where you're going."

As gently as I could, I put one leg over the saddle and lowered myself into the seat.

"This one girl. She very nice. Hold in front." Ibrahim pointed in front of me.

A large wooden peg thing was sticking out of the saddle so I clutched it tightly. After another moment's hesitation, Emily got on the other camel. Ibrahim clicked his tongue against his teeth and my camel stood.

I looked down and gulped.

Atallah was laughing.

"Are you okay Noor?" Salah asked. "You look scared."

I could hear the suppressed laughter in his voice. "I'm fine, it's just that – I mean, I didn't realise they would be so tall."

"You wanted to go for a camel ride," Emily said, still safely on the ground. Her camel was napping and ignoring Ibrahim's clicks.

"Yeah, well, they looked a lot smaller on the ground."

Ibrahim clicked his tongue and nudged Emily's camel a

few more times. With a low, rumbling growl the camel stood and huffed.

"I think mine is grumpy… " Emily said.

Ibrahim laughed and started singing.

"Atallah will follow us in jeep. I walk next to you," Salah said.

Ibrahim made a whistling noise through his teeth and the camels started moving.

"Let me down!" I yelped. "I changed my mind! I want to get off!"

Salah and Ibrahim erupted into laughter. Atallah was driving close by with his head out the window, also laughing.

"No, no you will enjoy it," Salah managed to say, still laughing.

The camel swayed like a desert ship, and my stomach swayed with her.

"I want to get off," I said, trying not to sound like I was panicking.

"This was your idea," Emily said, also laughing, from in front of me.

"Don't panic," Salah told me. "You will soon get used to it. Relax, enjoy."

I gritted my teeth and gripped the wooden horn as tightly as I could. Unlike Emily's camel could still be heard grumbling, my camel seemed calmer. After several metres of uneventful travel, I began to relax.

"I let them run now," Ibrahim said with a mischievous smile and dropped the rope tying the two camels together.

"Nooooo!" I screeched at him and Salah doubled over with laughter.

"Yes, I let them run." Ibrahim's laughter set off Atallah and Salah into a laughing fit.

"Oooha tistarji! *(Don't you dare!)*" I yelled a familiar childhood phrase in Arabic.

"Ibrahim, you in trouble now!" Atallah called from the car

window. "She yell at you in Arabic! Hahaha!" His laughter rang louder than the car engine.

Laughing, Ibrahim put up his hands in mock surrender and picked up the rope.

"Don't worry, I only joke." He turned his head toward Salah. "She speak Arabic with Lebanese accent."

I breathed a sigh of relief but didn't loosen my hold of the wooden horn.

Ibrahim was singing to the camels again, tugging at the rope every time Emily's camel stopped to nibble on a bit of dried shrub. I settled back into the saddle and tried to enjoy the swaying motion as the camel's hooves sank into the sand.

Just when I was getting the hang of it, Ibrahim brought the camels to a stop.

"Hold saddle tight Miss Emily and Miss Noor," Salah said. "Don't want you to fall off now at the end. When camel is on ground, then you climb off."

"Okay," Emily said in a cheerful tone. For someone who had been reluctant to try, she seemed to have enjoyed the ride more than me.

Ibrahim made some more clicking noises and whistles and my camel dropped her front legs.

"Eeeeeek!" I clutched the horn and pushed my bottom back firmly onto the saddle.

My camel had her bottom up in the air, with me hanging onto the saddle precariously and trying not to fly head first into the sand.

Breathless with laughter, Ibrahim tapped her back legs and she plonked down to the ground.

"Is ok, you can climb off now," Salah spluttered, wiping the tears from his eyes.

My fingers seemed frozen and my heart was hammering. Swallowing hard, I peeled them off the wooden horn and swung my leg over to slide off. My first few steps were unsteady and I preferred to think it was because I was adjusting from the swaying motion rather than trembling with fear.

Emily had glided off gracefully and stood next to Salah who was laughing so hard, tears were coming out of his eyes.

"Did you hear her scream? Like a little mouse?" Atallah said from the stationary jeep. "Like this – Eeeeeeeeeeeeeekkk."

"I did not! My voice is not that high pitched!"

"Eeeeeeeeeeeeeeeeeeeeeeeeeekkkk," Ibrahim imitated in a higher pitch.

"Eeeeeeeeeeeeeeeeeeeekk," Salah echoed.

Emily clutched her stomach, laughing helplessly.

A smile tugged at my lips. "Stop that! It's not funny?"

"Then why you laugh?" Atallah pointed to the traitorous grin that had spread across my face. "Is funniest thing I hear – Eeeeeeeeek!"

I rolled my eyes and climbed into the jeep.

"Thank you for the adventure Ibrahim," I waved from my seat.

"Welcome! Welcome!"

Salah and Emily climbed into the back and waved goodbye.

"Well, now you can relax and soon we have traditional Bedouin tea."

"That sounds lovely," Emily said.

"Is it far?" I asked.

"No, not far."

"Um, Salah …" I hesitated for a second. "Do you think …? I mean, would it be possible – could I drive some of the way?"

"What?" Emily turned to face me. "You want to drive the jeep?"

I shrugged my shoulders. "Well, I mean – I've ridden a camel and since I've already had one adventure, I thought maybe I could have another one and drive across the desert …"

Salah rubbed his palm over his carefully trimmed beard. "I don't know. If you want to drive, I ask Atallah and if he say yes, then you can. Is his car so I have to ask."

"It's ok if he says no, I just thought I would ask."

Salah nodded and knocked onto the back window to get Atallah's attention. A quick conversation and the jeep stopped.

"He say yes. Come, I will teach you to drive." Salah grinned and jumped out.

"Really? Thank you so much! By the way, I can drive."

"You know how to drive manual? That's great."

"Wait, what? Manual? I drive automatic."

Emily burst out laughing. "This will be fun."

"Is ok, you learn now." Atallah adjusted the white and red checked scarf around his head and leaned against the back of the jeep.

"Maybe this isn't such a good idea – I've never driven manual before… "

Salah looked at Atallah who nodded. "Is ok, I teach you. Very easy."

"If you're sure… "

I jumped over the back of the jeep and went to the driver's side. Salah had already taken his place as instructor in the passenger seat.

"Okay, so you know brake and accelerator. Now, these are gears."

I wiped my sweaty palms on my leggings and gulped.

There's so much to remember!

"Ready? Now turn on car."

"What? Already?"

"What you wait for?"

I could hear Atallah and Emily laughing from the back. Gritting my teeth I turned the key and the car shuddered.

"What happened? What was that?"

"Is okay, car stalled. Try again."

The jeep moved forward smoothly.

I shrieked. "I did it! I did it!"

"Keep going!" Salah shouted excitedly.

The jeep came to a shuddering halt.

"Try again."

I tried and tried. Sometimes the car would move a few centimetres before stalling. Salah started smacking his forehead. Emily and Atallah roared with laughter. I started sweating and grinding my teeth. Salah's voice was reaching new volumes. Atallah and Emily's laughter had reached the point of hysteria.

"I can't do it!" I wailed.

Salah sighed and shook his head. "Maybe we better stop before you ruin car."

We were moving forward but not smoothly.

Salah's door opened from the outside.

"You crazy?" Salah demanded.

Atallah was hanging from the side of the jeep with a big grin. "I teach now."

Salah threw up his hands in the air and climbed out to join Emily.

Atallah slid into the seat gracefully. "Is okay, relax. You just nervous."

"I can't do this, I will ruin your car – you should drive instead of me."

"It doesn't matter, everything can be fixed. I will teach you and you will drive."

"But I can't!"

"Yes you can, you are only afraid and Salah is too impatient with you. I will teach you."

"But what if I ruin it?" Apart from the repair costs, I didn't fancy having to walk all the way back to base in this heat.

"Doesn't matter. Everything can be fixed."

"No, I really don't think this is a good idea."

"Relax, I good teacher. You learn."

He started explaining what I had to do, in a very calm and laid back manner. I couldn't believe he wasn't worried about me ruining his car. Slowly, after much encouragement, I managed to start the car. And it didn't stall! Cheers erupted from the back of the jeep. Atalla grinned and patted my head.

Elated, I slowly edged forward.

"Go faster."

I pressed my foot on the pedal and we shot forward.

"Not that fast!" Emily yelled from the back.

"Sorry!" I shouted out the window and slowed down. I managed a few more meters, thrilled with my progress. "Thank you for letting me drive your car. I better stop now though."

"No, you do well. Keep driving."

I shook my head. "No, no. I've had enough for one day."

"No, you need practice. Keep driving. You focus on break and accelerator, I manage gears."

"Are you sure?"

He nodded and shifted gears. "Go a little faster."

I gripped the steering wheel and steered the car across the sand, grateful there was no traffic or any animals I could potentially hit. Emily and Salah had stopped laughing so I took it as a sign that my driving had improved and leaned back in the driver's seat.

Atallah chatted, asking about my name and background. Like everyone else I had met on the trip so far, he seemed to find my mixed heritage surprising.

"They say the most beautiful ones are mixed."

I felt something on my knee and looked down to find his hand resting there.

Cheeky little bastard!

I looked at him with narrowed eyes, glaring as hard as I could.

Blushing slightly, he snatched his hand away and focused on the gears. "Turn wheel left, we almost at Bedouin camp."

I followed the instructions and a few meters later a large black tent appeared.

"Stop over here," Atallah indicated to a spot in front of the tent.

I undid my seat belt. "Thank you so much for letting me drive! I think I'll sit in the back later though, I've had enough driving for one day."

Atallah laughed and nodded.

THE TENT WAS SET up as a large rectangle leaving the front completely open. It was as large as a small apartment and thick black fabric managed to block out most of the Sun.

Salah and Atallah walked right in and greeted the Bedouin man with a hug.

Emily and I stood just outside of the tent waiting to be invited in.

"Welcome!" The Bedouin man opened his arms wide. "Please come in."

We mumbled thanks and walked into the surprisingly cool tent. I sniffed the air appreciatively. A hint of spices and freshly brewed tea drifted past my nose.

"Hello! What's your name?" Emily said in the voice she reserved for greeting cats.

A lovely ginger cat was weaving between her legs and purring.

"Look," I pointed under the table. "There's a kitten sleeping."

Like every other time I saw an animal on this trip, I thought of my fur kids at home and missed them. *I'll see them soon,* I told myself and caressed the ginger cat in front of me.

Salah and Atallah were happily chatting to our Bedouin host who prepared the tea and served it to us in beautiful glasses. Despite the heat, it was surprisingly refreshing.

Emily leaned in and whispered, "Do you think we should buy something?"

I looked at the large table covered with trinkets, costume jewellery and cosmetic creams. "It feels like we are expected to buy something, or they wouldn't have gone to so much trouble to display it."

"Yeah," Emily agreed. "I'll buy some jewellery for my mum."

I nodded and choose a necklace and a small pot of amber cream for my mum. At this rate, she would be able to open her own jewellery store.

As soon as we finished our tea, Salah ushered us back to the jeep so we could start our long drive back to Amman.

I SQUIRMED UNCOMFORTABLY in the seat. The cars air-conditioning was working overtime but seemed to make little difference in the blistering heat.

"Salah, how much longer until we get to Amman?"

"Two more hours."

"I won't last that long. Is there a public toilet somewhere I could use?" All the liquid I had drank so far was making its presence felt.

"Is that a public toilet?" Emily pointed to a little square building further ahead.

"Yes, but we won't stop there."

"Why not? I really need to go!"

"Is fine for Jordanians but not tourists. Don't worry, I take you to a much cleaner place not far from here. They also have food so you can eat something."

"Fine, but please drive faster and get us there quickly."

Salah laughed and stepped on the accelerator.

After what seemed like a long time, Salah parked in front of a large square building. I jumped out of the car and ran inside. Thankfully, the bathroom was easy to find and very clean. With that taken care of, my stomach growled loudly. I found Emily browsing the shelves outside the bathroom.

"What is this place?"

"It's a stop for tourists on the way to Amman. Salah said

we can do some shopping if we want, and we can get some lunch here too," Emily said.

"I don't think I can fit any more souvenirs in my suitcase."

"I'll make room," Emily said with determination. "I've already found dead sea products and Israeli glass for much, much cheaper!"

"Really? Are you sure it's authentic Israeli glass?"

"That's what it says on there and it looks the same. Come have a look."

I followed her across the store, past shelves full of fabric toy camels and Bedouin dolls in beautifully embroidered gowns, as well as dolls wearing long flowing gowns with only their embroidered eyes visible. The area she took me to what is dedicated to dead sea products and cosmetics. The shelves next to it with full of blown glass objects with colourful swirly patterns. They looked just like the Israeli glass goblet I bought in Jerusalem for 90 shekels, except here six small glasses were being sold for 10 Dineri.

"I thought you weren't going to buy any more souvenirs?"

"These are very small, I'm sure I can fit them in my suitcase," I told her.

Emily laughed and followed me to the cash register, her shopping basket fuller than mine.

We found Salah in the cafe section of the store. The choice of food was very limited to sandwiches that didn't look very fresh or appetising. The ice cream fridge was empty and the shelves were bare of everything except for a couple of packets of chips and biscuits. Salah was keen to continue our journey back to the capital so we ordered a couple of sandwich wraps and ate them in the car.

The long drive continued. Salah sped past some soldiers signalling for a lift, explaining that although Jordanians felt a duty to offer soldiers a lift, he wouldn't because we were in the car and he was responsible for our protection. I didn't really understand what he meant and I was too distracted preparing his tip in an envelope without him noticing because today was the last day we would see him. He would drop us off at the hotel, and tomorrow morning Omar would take us to the airport.

"Here we are," Salah announced cheerfully, parking in front of the same hotel we had stayed at on our first night in Jordan. "I take your bags inside and organize your room then say goodbye."

"Okay, thanks," Emily said and got out of the car.

I hid the envelope with money in my scarf and followed her through the luggage check.

"I hope this time they give us a non-smoking room," I muttered.

"Okay, your room is ready and you will have breakfast before Omar come get you tomorrow morning. All is organized. He take you to airport and help you check in, then Inshallah (God willing) you have safe trip."

"Thank you for all your help, you've been a wonderful tour guide," Emily told him.

"Yes, and thank you for letting us take our time – especially with shopping."

Salah grinned. "You are very welcome! I hope you enjoy tour and come again to Jordan."

I pulled out the envelope with the tip and handed it to him. "This is for you, to thank you for being a good tour guide."

"Oh, thank you so much, thank you. It has been pleasure Miss Emily and Miss Noor. Have a safe trip home."

"Thank you, goodbye," Emily waved.

"Thanks again. Bye," I waved as he walked through the doors.

"I wonder if we tipped him too much?" Emily said as we stepped into the lift.

"No idea. I never know how much to tip, but I did leave money to tip Omar too."

"Do we have any other Jordanian dineri left?"

"A little if we want to buy food at the airport."

"Want to have a look at the little souvenir shop downstairs? It's open now, and it wasn't last time we were here."

I laughed. "Fine, we can have a look before dinner."

The room was an improvement, away from the main street chaos and noise and it didn't stink of smoke. The TV didn't work but we were too busy packing and repacking our suitcases to make everything fit, so it wasn't a problem. A few more little trinkets from the souvenir shop (bracelets to protect from the evil eye and a small carved stone camel) which could be easily stuffed in hand luggage, and a buffet dinner finished our last evening in Jordan.

CHAPTER 18
A FOND FAREWELL

After a quick breakfast Omar drove us to the airport. It was chaotic, people everywhere you looked except those we actually needed – like the flight check-in attendants. We waited in line, or at least Emily and I tried to, while Omar kept nudging our suitcases forward. Cheerfully greeting a check-in attendant who had appeared behind the counter, he checked us in before other passengers, wished us a safe flight and left as soon as he had received his tip.

I turned to Emily who was checking her boarding pass. "What do you want to do for the next couple of hours?"

"We could look at the shops and then have some lunch before boarding?"

"I wonder if the sales assistants remember us from our first time?" I grinned. "They must have thought we were crazy walking around in circles without realising it!"

Emily laughed. "I want to have a look at the prices of the Dead Sea products here. I'm pretty sure I got them cheaper at that place Salah stopped at on the way back to Amman, but I might find something on sale here."

"Sure, go ahead. I'll browse too."

We took our time looking at the merchandise in the shops and when it was close to lunchtime we went to the same café where we had our first Middle Eastern falafel. It seemed like a fitting way to end the trip. In a way it was a complete circle. Just like the airport. I was back where I had started my great adventure to Israel and Jordan, only this time I had many happy memories and was, hopefully, a little less of the naïve traveller.

"I'm going to miss the falafels here," I mourned after finishing the last bite.

"Me too! But maybe we can find an authentic Israeli or Jordanian restaurant in Melbourne."

"Come on." I stood up and pulled on my backpack. "We better start heading towards the check in gate."

I was torn between excitement to see my family, both human and animal, and sad that the adventure was over, but the closer I got to the plane the more my excitement grew. I couldn't wait to give them their presents and show them pictures of my trip. I especially couldn't wait to cuddle my little Susu and Bruli.

We found our seats and stored our carry on in the compartment above and settled in for a long flight. Emily fell asleep with her headphones on and I wasn't in the mood to watch a movie so I started reading the memoir I had bought at Petra, but I couldn't concentrate. I was too distracted, one second thinking about my family and the next of all the things I had seen and people I had met. Restless, I pulled out my travel journal and flicked through my entries – exploring ancient cities, finding bargains at local markets, getting lost, enjoying local food, riding a camel in the desert... There were so many wonderful memories to take home with me.

Not every memory was pleasant though. Some people had been kind and generous and others had tried to take advantage of us as tourists, whether out of poverty or greed I don't know. I had travelled a long way from home thinking I was exploring a very different world to my own, and in some ways it was, but in many other ways it wasn't. The languages, food, customs and way of life was different but these are all superficial things.

I was born in Lebanon, spent part of my childhood in Italy and grew up in Australia. They were three very different countries but one thing had become very clear to me. We are all essentially the same. We all share the same physical and emotional needs for things like food, water, love, and peace. We all experience moments of fear, joy, tranquillity, and enlightenment. We fear what we do not know or understand, and we pursue paths that will secure our wellbeing and happiness. The landscape, weather, social and political context might change – but human nature is the same everywhere.

DEAR READER

Thank you for reading!

If you liked this book, have a look at my other travel memoirs. They can be read on their own and in any order, and they are available as ebooks and paperback. If you prefer to read in chronological order, here is my suggestion

Big Cities and Mountain Villages

Falafels and Bedouins

Christmas Lights and Carnevale

If you have a minute, please consider leaving a review on your favorite social media platform. Readers trust other readers, and reviews are the lifeblood for writers.

Enjoy photos of my travels at

https://www.facebook.com/NoorDeOlinad/

Made in the USA
Las Vegas, NV
07 January 2023

65112514R00152